KONTAKION

FOR YOU DEPARTED

2 | 1

ALAN PATON

JONATHAN CAPE
THIRTY BEDFORD SQUARE
LONDON

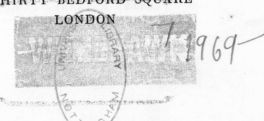

1969

FIRST PUBLISHED 1969
© 1969 BY ALAN PATON

JONATHAN CAPE LTD,
30 BEDFORD SQUARE, LONDON WC1

SBN   224 61716 8

PRINTED AND BOUND IN GREAT BRITAIN BY
BUTLER & TANNER LTD,
FROME AND LONDON

For David and Jonathan

KONTAKION: a hymn for one departed

1

The boys went back to Johannesburg on the afternoon of Sunday. The date was October 22nd, 1967, but you did not know it. They went back to arrange their affairs, but they knew they would be returning soon. Ray Swart took them to the airport so that I could stay with you. To my surprise he returned about six, and said, *this is the time you always have your drink, and I thought you might like company.* I half thought of offering him a drink in the lounge, because on your face could be seen the imminence of death. Yet I had sat in your room, our room, ever since the day you could no longer leave it.

So we sat in your room. I wondered if I should have brought in a screen. But I didn't. When Ray had gone, Queenie came on duty, and said to me, *father, I'm going to sit in the room tonight.* I got up four times to look at the oxygen. You were breathing shallowly but easily, not with that painful exertion, that terrible rhythm, like a box rising, staying up a moment, then falling with a bang till it rose again, a spasm that made the heart of the watcher fit to break. It was as though nature, having struck you the second and irremediable blow, withdrew her attention from the first affliction.

At six in the morning I looked at the oxygen for the fourth time. Then I slept. At five minutes to seven Queenie called me and said, *father she's gone.* And you had gone too, oh most brave and faithful one. I kissed your still warm face, and said, *sleep well my love*. I prayed, *may her soul rest in peace*. I did not weep. I set about the business of preparing your funeral.

2

When did I first meet you? I would think some time in February 1925, on the tennis-court in Ixopo. I remember you as something like an urchin, full of mischief and zest and repartee, playing with all your heart, triumphant in victory and determined in defeat. You were twenty-eight, and married, to a man that your family had not wanted you to marry, because his tuberculosis was far advanced. I was twenty-two, a young, eager, clear-eyed virgin, full of mischief and zest like yourself. I was a teacher at the Ixopo High School, whose staff, except for old Mrs Humphreys, were all young like myself.

Your sister Rad was twenty-six. You were worried that she was not married, and I think you would have liked us to fall in love. You asked us both to dinner at your house, but if you had such expectations, they were not advanced that evening. When we had gone, your husband said to you, *that youngster's in love with you*. What you replied, I cannot now remember. But what he said was true.

In what sense was it true? It was for one thing the purest love in the world, for it did not desire to possess you. I do not remember that I ever thought of touching you; I certainly did not ever try to touch you. I, not knowing it fully, had given my heart into your hands. Although I laughed and teased you on the tennis-court, I was virginal and shy. I have a picture taken of me at that time. There was no guile in that face.

3

I first rang the doctor, then our sons. I said to them, *Mrs P. has gone,* because that name was used by them even more affectionately than Mum. Then I rang all our close friends. I asked the doctor to let the under-takers come at 9.30, because I wanted Elizabeth to see you. I asked Theresa, Anna, Zikali and Alfred if they would like to see you — because your body was still you to me — and they came in solemnly, and Theresa and Anna wept. At 9.0 Elizabeth came, and hurried to see you, and I pulled down the sheet that the doctor had pulled up over your face, and she cried out at you in Afrikaans, *slaap gerus, my nooi, sleep well, my mis-tress.* To me she said, *Ons kan niks doen nie, dis God wat alles doen, We can do nothing, it is God who does it all.*

They took you away at 9.30, and I watched you go. Or should I say, I watched your coffin go? Whatever I say, some great change has come over me and this house and this life, and all those years together, and all those journeys and those holidays, and the family games, and the dinners at The George and Salvador's on special occasions, and our parties at the house which

were like no other parties that I ever went to, have
come to an end. One can hardly believe it, and one can
hardly disbelieve it, because the bed is empty where
you lay so long.

4

New Year's Day. The first New Year since 1926 that
you have not been with me (except for four occasions
when I was away). They all say to me *a happy New
Year*.

Dennis brought your photograph yesterday. You
didn't like it, but I do. It is the face of someone who
knows suffering, grave and strong. It is there where it
ought to be, with mine, and those of your sons and
daughters-in-law and grandchildren. This picture is
very different from the one above my bed, which I
would guess was taken thirty years ago. You look very
sweet; the suffering was yet to come.

My mind goes back to other pictures. There was one
of you in your mourning clothes. And another of you
in a brown-and-white check dress, your first relaxation
of the grim black rule of an age that is gone for ever. I
wish I could find them, for those were the days of my
first love.

I went to Ixopo in February 1925, and played tennis
and bridge with you, and had dinner at your house.
Then on May 24th, which was then called Empire Day,
I went home to Pietermaritzburg for the short holidays. On May 25th, there happened an event which in

great measure determined my life. Your husband died.

How I heard, I cannot now remember. What I thought, I cannot now remember. I cannot even remember if I thought I should like to marry you. Nor can I remember what I said to you when I saw you again. I cannot even remember if I called you by your Christian name.

But I remember the grim black clothes. You were back at Morningview, your childhood home, and you would walk past the school, and past the house where you and your husband lived, to the office where you worked. Marjorie said to me, *why does Dorrie wear those terrible clothes?* I was silent, but my heart was in your defence. Although I write it myself, how pure was my love.

Nor can I remember if I saw you at all, or if you went away. In July I went away myself for the school holiday, and did not see you till I returned in August.

5

After they had taken you away, I still slept in our room. I said my prayers at your bed, but I find that the empty bed does not mean much to me. It is the empty house that shouts at me, the empty desolate silent house, the house where you are not, the house where you would be waiting for me to return from some journey or other. Those times I shall always remember, for they were the times when you openly showed your love and pleasure. You did not do so very often, because there was a touch of austerity in your nature.

That first evening Pat and Sakuntala brought dinner up for me. We talked about you mostly. They were a great comfort to me.

6

When I returned to Ixopo School in August 1925, you asked me to coach your sister Ruth in mathematics. Ruth was sixteen and very shy, and you used to tease her about me, which embarrassed her extremely. Your father and mother and Rad were in England, and I visited Morningview more and more often. Yet I cannot remember what I called you.

One thing I *do* remember, and that is that we enjoyed being with each other. You spent more of your time with me than with anyone except Ruth and Garry. One evening in the little room where I coached Ruth you decided to read my hands. You announced that my character was strong, but I cannot remember anything else, only that my hands were in your hands. You knew that of course, but you did not know my heart was there also.

What were you doing, reading my hands? You never again read any person's hands as far as I remember. As for me, I did not try to touch you at all. My love grew deeper and deeper, but I did not try to show it. I suppose it was looking out of those guileless eyes. Did you know? Did you not remember that you were a one-month widow, and that you were a woman who had loved and I was a boy who had not? And you were a woman who had loved much, because you married against your mother's will, and if you were afraid of any person in your life, that person was your mother. Did you know what you were doing?

7

October 24th, 1967. The telegrams are pouring in, six, ten at a time, almost every hour. My heart is filled with grief and pride.

In the evening I had dinner with Dennis and Devi, and then went to the airport to meet our sons. We sat up till 2.0 a.m. talking about you.

For whom do we grieve, for ourselves, or for the one we have lost? That is what your friend Amabel in New Zealand has asked me. I am going to write to her that I grieved for you often these last two years, and for myself sometimes, but that now I grieve for myself alone.

The first time I grieved for you was in September 1965, when we were staying with Ruth Hayman in Johannesburg. Your distress, your unending struggle for breath, was a bitter thing to see. But the first deep grief came in January 1967, when the doctor told me that you had a hypostatic pneumonia, a permanent pneumonia that you were not strong enough to get rid of, that might one day flare up and carry you away.

That evening as I drove back from King George V

Hospital, I was seized by spasm after spasm of grief. They would rise up from some place inside me, into my throat it seemed, some incredible compound of ache and pain; then the tears blinded me. But that grief was for you also, that your brave life was ending. For you, so hopeful, so eager, so determined to do without the oxygen, so determined to have a real bath again. For me, knowing it could never be.

8

September 19th, 1925. I had dinner at Morningview and after that we sat by the fire. Mrs Cox went to bed. How long did we sit there? Till the early hours of September 20th. You left your chair and sat on the floor. Then you complained that it was uncomfortable. Then I, with incredible courage, suggested that you should rest your back against my knees. And you did so. But I, with an incredible cowardice that followed hard on the heels of my incredible courage, did no more than put my hands on my knees. Then you, impatient perhaps, put your hand up to adjust the collar of your blouse, and our hands met, and my arms were around you, and my head was pressed against yours, and your face was upturned, and we kissed, and I said *I love you* and you said *I love you too.* How long I stayed after that, I do not remember. When at last I left, you walked along the veranda with me, and when you kissed me good night, you pressed yourself against me in a way that no one had ever done before. And I, knowing you to be a chaste woman, knew what it was to be loved.

The other things were left unspoken. Except for one, and that was that our love must be kept a secret for some time, out of respect for the decencies of those days.

And I walked home like a man to whom a door has opened so that he may look into heaven.

9

October 25th, 1967. The telegrams pour in, now from Canada and the United States and Great Britain and Italy. Your funeral service is to be at 3.0 p.m. The only flowers are to be from me, and David and Nancy, and Jonathan and Margaret. I go into the garden and see the St Joseph's lilies that you always said I was too mean to cut. Then I said to myself, why am I ordering flowers? I cancelled the order, and cut the flowers I was too mean to cut. Mrs Coles made them up for me as a gift. She gave me a card too, and I wrote on it, 'from Alan, with love and thanks'.

And that is what I do. I give thanks for the blessings of our life, for a love that persisted through vicissitudes, for a love of others that triumphed over the barriers of race and custom and was given to any person who wanted it or was in need of it, and which was so abundantly returned – good measure, pressed down, shaken together, and running over, shall men give into your bosom – that is the truth. But it happens only when you give yourself with your gift. That is why so many people loved you.

10

September 20th, 1925. How can I teach today? How does one come down from heaven? How does one look when the whole of one's life has been transfigured? Yet no one saw the aura of celestial light. Although I taught as usual, although half of my mind was applied steadily to my work, the other half was occupied by the stupendous thought that you loved me, and that you had come to love me at what seemed the most unlikely time. And also by the ecstatic thought that at 9.0 p.m. when I came off duty at the boy's hostel, I would be going to see you. I wish I could remember how you looked when at last I came, and what you said, but I cannot.

Bliss, that is the word I suppose, for those far-off days. During the first week-end that I was not on duty, I spent most of the time with you. My Sunday supper you cooked yourself, and I have never forgotten the joy of being waited on by you. I had never lacked for the love of family and friends, but this was something of my own, not to be shared with any other. Mrs Cox watched it all, with approval I should think. Did we tell anyone else? Did you tell Ruth? When did people begin to know?

One afternoon you and your cousin Alwyn and I walked along the Highflats road to the hospital of Christ the King. When we reached there we sat on a bank and it was either you or Alwyn who wrote on the ground with a stick, your initials, D.O.L. Then Alwyn scratched out the L and substituted a P, with a knowing kind of chuckle. I may have blushed, but I was also filled with pride.

11

At a quarter to three David and Jonathan and I left for the church. I was quite calm till we crossed the new bridge and turned towards St Agnes. Then the sight of the cars packed into the church grounds threatened to unman me, but it did not. Then there was the church itself packed with people of all the nations under our sun, just the kind of company you would have wished to be about you. On your coffin was the spray of St Joseph's lilies, one of the most beautiful of all white flowers.

After the introductory sentences we sang the 23rd Psalm, and Archbishop Paget read the verses beginning 'And I saw a new heaven and a new earth'. After that the Botha's Hill Settlement choir sang 'Jesu, Lover of my Soul', which I chose for you.

Then the Archbishop spoke. He had difficulty in getting into the pulpit, and it was clear that his knees were giving him great pain. Murray Dell wanted him to speak from the steps, but he would not. He was doing a big thing, and he wanted to do it properly. Amongst other things he said:

For their partnership in Alan's literary work; for their gracious and generous hospitality to all peoples; for their heroic holding firm to their Christian con-

victions, for their courageous sharing of one another's anxieties and frustrations; and in those later days in sickness, distress, and suffering; we thank God.

After he had spoken, Murray read the sentences beginning 'Man that is born of a woman hath but a short time to live', and among the prayers he included 'Make me, O Lord, the instrument of Thy peace'. Then we all sang with great vigour, 'Now thank we all our God'. There were many there who mourned for you, but it was above all else a service of thanksgiving.

After the benediction they wheeled your coffin to the door, and David, Jonathan, Murray and I carried it to the hearse. So ended the most wonderful funeral service that I ever attended.

12

The halcyon days. I write of them with unbelievable longing to have again what one cannot have again, so that my desire to relive what cannot be relived begins actually to war against my knowledge, final and ineluctable, that it cannot be done. It is a strange thing to happen to me who have always tried to live by reason. And I know it for a kind of madness, and I can imagine what it might do to someone who has not the power to resist it. For ultimately I do not desire to live in any past, though I understand that some so desire it that in the end they do it.

Part of my longing is for myself, for my youth, for

the days of my first love. But part of it is longing for you, and for those days when there was no joy greater than that of belonging to you, and of having you belong to me, and of being taken into your life, and learning your thoughts and your jokes and your ambitions, and being shown, cautiously and gradually, to your friends. You did this so warmly that I was filled with pride, knowing that some might censure you for loving so soon again.

You told me that you had been a believing and practising Christian, but that your husband had had no religious belief, and that you had ceased to believe and to worship. But you hoped that I would help you to recover your faith. Thank God I did not attempt to instruct you or argue with you, for even in the days of my young manhood I believed that this was the most barren way of communicating faith. So I attempted to communicate faith to you by loving you, wholeheartedly and tenderly, and as unselfishly as I knew how. It was given to me to be generous in love, but now I surpassed myself, and to you to whom desolation had come so suddenly it was like a reparation, and you warmed to me in gratitude.

And all these memories are bound up with the love I felt for the place in which you were born. In those days the Ixopo countryside was one of rolling hills of grass, fed and kept green by the rains and the mists. Many of the boys and girls of the school came from these green and rolling farms, Annarth and Loch Buighe and Benmore and Waterford. Many a time I walked over the hills to these farms, sometimes in a world of mist, through grass and bracken, and hearing the titihoya crying. A schoolmaster is usually held in respect by the people of a farming community, mostly I suppose because he is thought to be learned. It was my first experience of this kind of world, and I entered into its life eagerly. No woman's birthplace was ever adopted more wholeheartedly by her lover than yours by me. And the village too. How I wish you could read these words!

The halcyon days. And that means not only the sweetest days of life, it means also the days that cannot be lived again, except in memory.

13

It was my wish to stand with David and Jonathan outside the church after the service, to meet those who wished to speak to us. This is a sound and proper wish, and a practical thing to do, for the comfort of it is quite immeasurable. It was an experience like no other in my life, and the memory of it is as intense as the memory of that far-off day when I first embraced you. My sister Dorrie wrote to me that the church was filled with love, and the words may sound trite but what other words can be used? And outside the church it enveloped us, filling me with such a pride that grief — visible grief — was held at bay. The Archbishop had said that for you it must have been a triumphant passing as you went forth to join that band of those who have fought the good fight and have finished the course and have kept the faith and have won the peace.

And so it was. And what made it triumphant was that you, in this country of fear and division, were loved by so many people of so many kinds and conditions. And this love included me also — it was our work and our home and our peace — and pride and thankfulness kept grief in its place. Fatima, from her height of five-foot-nothing, reached up her arms and pulled my head down to hers, and this action, regarded with such distaste by so many white South Africans, is beyond judgment in the presence of death. It should be beyond judgment in the presence of love also, but it is not so.

I venture to think that some people, who had drawn away from us over the years because of our opinions and actions, and who would have been shocked at the sight of my being embraced by women not white, were now overwhelmed by it, and saw with new eyes that what they had considered a shame was in fact a glory.

When at last they had all gone, Murray Dell took us to the crematorium and committed your body to the fire. They asked if I wanted your ashes, and I said *No*. They asked if I wanted a plaque in the Garden of Remembrance, and I said No. I don't want a plaque in the church; in any event for some reason St Agnes has no plaques. But I told the Archbishop that I wished there were a wall somewhere in the grounds of St Agnes where one could place a plaque. He said he would speak to the Rector about it. That is what I shall do if it is permitted. I don't quite know why. I think it must be because I want there to be some evidence that you once lived upon the earth, and loved and were loved.

Sleep well, my love.

Give rest, O Christ, to thy servant with thy saints: where sorrow and pain are no more, neither sighing, but life everlasting. Thou only art immortal, the Creator and Maker of man: and we are mortal formèd of the earth, and unto earth shall we return: for so thou didst ordain when thou createdest me, saying, Dust thou art, and unto dust shalt thou return. All we go down to the dust; and weeping o'er the grave, we make our song, alleluya, alleluya.

Give rest, O Christ, to thy servant with thy saints: where sorrow and pain are no more, neither sighing, but life everlasting.*

So do I weep over the grave, and make my song, alleluya, alleluya, alleluya.

14

Ah, what did I do wrong? Was I too importunate, or too possessive? Or was the guilt of your so-soon loving oppressing you? I can see you now, standing by the same fireplace in front of which you had not long before acknowledged your love for me. And you said to me, so far as I can remember, *there is one thing you must understand clearly, and that is that I shall never love you as I loved my husband.*

I cannot remember that I said anything. I let my-

* This is the Russian Kontakion of the Departed.

self out on to that same veranda where you had pressed yourself against me, and walked down the dark lampless road to the boys' hostel where I lived. The hostel was in darkness, and I let myself into my room, and went to bed with my misery. I did not think of the future, all I could think of was the pain of the present. You had suddenly become a woman I had not seen before, for the one I had known was tender and loving and teasing and warm. And this one was a woman speaking to a boy, a woman of the world speaking to an innocent, explaining to him that he must not presume to think that his love for her could be matched by hers for him.

Yet perhaps I am wrong, and you were speaking, not out of experience, but out of ignorance of the nature of love. For in true love one gives oneself, and it does not matter if one has given oneself before. If I were to marry again, and for love, I would give myself again, and I would say to the woman, I have given myself before, and now I give myself again, with no withholding, and will love and cherish you. But I am writing now at the age of sixty-four and you were speaking then at the age of twenty-eight, not knowing that if loves are to be compared, one does not tell one's lover, unless of course he is the winner of the competition.

I did not think of these things in my hostel room. I was a mass of pain, like a whipped creature. Yet one thing I had resolved, and that was never to go to your home again. It was not so much a resolve as a realization that I could never look at you again. I do not remember any anger, I do not remember thinking that my love was ended, I remember only the realization that I could not speak to you again.

Then the door of the room was opened and shut again. And you were at the side of the bed, weeping and loving, and asking to be forgiven and being forgiven.

Just what was said, I cannot now remember. I cannot remember if you said that you would love me with all the love that was in your power to give. It seems to me that the joy of reconciliation overshadowed the need for talking. It was a mistake of course, but I was a boy of twenty-two being comforted by the one who had wounded me, and it would have been beyond all my powers for me to have said to you, *now let us decide once and for all where we stand*.

Yet even joy has to be sensible. There you were in my room, and at a late hour, and if we had been found there it is almost certain I would have been dismissed and you disgraced. I don't think the story of your urgent need to comfort and be forgiven would have weighed much with the authorities, not in the year 1925. But how were you to go, that was the question? If you left alone and were seen, that would not be much better than if we left together and were seen. In the end I left the room first, and having decided that the whole hostel was sound asleep, I went back to the room and told you that all was clear. When you had been gone a minute, and no outraged inspectors of schools had appeared, I slipped out myself, and together we walked up the dark road to Morningview.

That evening had one consequence. It made it impossible for us ever to speak of your husband again. I did not speak of him again till 1966, the year before you died. Jonathan was staying with us, and he asked why we should have two table-napkin rings, one marked 'D' and the other 'B'. And you would not answer him. It was I who said to him, *that is the initial of your mother's first husband.* Jonathan was astonished, and he said, *you're not serious? Are you joking?* I said, *he died, and three years later I married your mother.* But you did not add a word. Later you said to Margaret, *there was nothing scandalous about it.*

What strange creatures we humans are! Just how we come to love one another, and to care for one another for all of our common life, and to grant one another territories on which the other does not trespass, and to bear with one another's foibles and weaknesses, and to grow closer and closer till we have but one mind on all the things that matter to us most, and to have children, and to put their happiness and their welfare above all other things, and to give them safety and security until it is proper for them to find these things for themselves, how it ever comes to happen in this imperfect world, only God knows.

15

The flood of telegrams begins to abate, but now begins the flood of letters. Letters are quite different from telegrams, they can make one weep. They come ten, twenty a day, and they are going to come for weeks before the flood begins to abate.

When the post comes, I sit and read them, and weep over them, especially those that speak of your warmth and your courage, of your solicitude and your wit. Some people write that you were a match for me in repartee, which is undoubtedly meant as a compliment to us both. One day when I was reading, the irreversibility and the irrevocability of it all suddenly caused me to burst into sobbing, and the one fit led to another, and the second to a third. That was grief, pure and simple, of itself entire, uncompounded with either pride or thanks. The last time I sobbed was in my office at Diepkloof Reformatory, on the day I left it, June 30th, 1948, and Mr Verwey heard me, and came and closed the door.

Now today, eleven weeks after your death, comes a letter from Norman in prison, and I weep again. He writes to me:

You know better than anyone how well Mrs P. was loved and why. I've been trying lately to capture for myself what it was about her that made so many of us so fond of her. I think it was that she seemed to be a blend of loved elder sister and mother. We did not stand in awe of her but at the same time we respected her. She was gay, she was natural, she was fun, and she could be frivolous (I'm thinking particularly of those verses she and Walter used to exchange), but she also had great moral force. She didn't cultivate dignity yet she had dignity, and I think she was able to be gay and what an aunt of mine would have called 'cheeky' because she knew, without vanity, that

.–[26]–.

she was staunch and fine in the important things. What you said about her to Maurice sums up her quality better than anything I can say. She was resolutely loyal. She went your road – not an easy one – with willingness, courage, and it seems to me, ungrudging love. Yeats, in that lovely poem of his, Easter 1916, says 'Too long a sacrifice can make a stone of the heart'. But nothing in this life could have made a stone of Mrs P.'s heart. It was too warm and vital. She loved people and enjoyed them. Her strength came (so I believe) not from denying the bad, but from affirming the good, which is why young people (who feel their flawed characters keenly, whatever they might pretend) loved and honoured her, and liked to be near her.

I know something of your strength Mr P., but I know too that strength doesn't make grief easier to endure. Please know that all of your friends think of you often and with love. Leo and Maurice know I'm writing and send love.

To me these words are perfect. The gaiety, the fun and what Norman's aunt would have called 'cheekiness' – that is how I remember you on the tennis-court at Ixopo. Of your moral strength I was to learn later. But it was your cheekiness that made me lose my heart to you. And how jealous I was when you were cheeky to others! How you used to tease that shy young Jock who worked on your brother's farm, and how you would put on a Scottish accent when you spoke to him! It wouldn't surprise me to learn that he fell in love with you too. He was tongue-tied and earnest, and used to look at you (so I thought) out of worshipping eyes. I cannot remember well, but I think I expostulated with you (was that out of jealousy, or out of concern for Jock?). And I think (how I wish I could remember these things!) you stopped it, but whether that was out of concern for me or for Jock, it is now too late to discover.

Gradually I lost all jealousy and accepted the cheekiness as part of your nature. And I can see you at the door welcoming our friends, a woman with a smile and affection, and a man with that gay teasing look in your eyes. Sex, no doubt, but wonderful.

Together with Norman's letter came one from Krishna Shah, who says Los Angeles is an island, and he did not know of your death till he went to New York.

I can't believe the news about Dori. Her exuberant laughter echoes in my ears and her gestures of warmth are vivid before my eyes. And I am speechless with the news. I am enraged with the angel of death.

But he would not have been enraged had he seen that unending struggle to breathe.

Norman in his letter refers to what I said to Maurice about you. What I wrote to Maurice I wrote first to your friend Amabel in New Zealand. I said that you were courageous (with fears); tolerant (with intolerances); loving (with prickles); loyal (without disloyalties); honest (without dishonesties).

It is not every man who finds treasure on a tennis-court.

16

My birthday today. David and Nancy, Jonathan and Margaret, and the grandchildren are here. Christopher is sleeping in our room, in your bed. I cannot remember when you started giving me a birthday party, but I do remember the thought and time and labour that you put into it. It was one of your generous gifts. After you died I decided that I would give it again, partly because I wanted to have all our friends around me, partly because you would have wished it to be so. I knew that everyone there would remember the party of a year ago, when you sat in the big chair near the door to receive your guests, so brave and ill. And so they did remember, not with constraint, only with love.

There is one thing you would have been angry about. You were angry the first time I asked more than fifty guests, and last year when I asked more than sixty. Well, this year I have asked more than ninety, and it is your own doing, because these extra people are the ones who came into our lives during this bitter year and were so generous to us.

What do I mean, you would have been *angry*? Was it anger? No, it was more a kind of sharpness. You would say, *you know, Alan, it really makes me angry*, and I would go to you to soothe you, and you would push me away and say, *no, I won't be pacified by that.* Then in due course you would recover.

You could be sharp with the boys too. You would be angry with Jonathan when he was small and give him a good smart smack. Then he would be angry too. But when I came back in ten minutes the pair of you would be billing and cooing.

You were very sharp about their frequent visits to Kloof in 1967, when you were in hospital. You thought they were being extravagant. I told you that you were wrong, and that they came because they loved you, and you were ill and they wanted to see you. But I could not tell you that they had a knowledge, hidden from you, that your life was drawing to its end.

This sharpness was part of your nature, and all your family knew it and were not alienated by it. And it was a clean sharpness, with nothing mean about it. I think it came from your mother, a kind of Scottish trait, not a dourness, rather a kind of ruggedness, which prevented you often from showing your affection. I remember the night when Doctor O. telephoned to say that my mother had just died. You put your arms about me, and drew my head down to yours with fierceness, and said to me, *you know your mother and I never exchanged an angry word.* At such times you quite conquered me, and I wished you could have done it more often. But you did not, for it was not your nature. That was a difference between us, for I am demonstrative by nature, and you were not. But I shall tell of other times when you conquered me.

17

I remember one event of the time when your husband
was still alive. Two sisters from the Hospital of Christ
the King came to the school hostel where I was living,
asking for donations to their work. I gave them half-a-
crown, or five shillings, I cannot remember, and signed
my name on their list. That evening I went to Morningview, and you and Rad, with unconcealed glee, pro-
duced the subscription list, and handed me back my
donation. You had played the same trick on your
father, and you gave him back his donation also. I
cannot remember whether you said to Rad, or Rad
said to you, *Alan (or Mr Paton) is too cocky, and we'll
take him down a peg or two.* I should add that I was
not very bright on that occasion because it happened
to be All Fools' Day. What is more, you deliberately
traded on my weakness, knowing that I would never
dream of suspecting a woman dressed as a nun. How
pleased you were with yourself! What a look of
triumph on your face!

18

The party is over. Ninety-seven people, isn't that
shocking! Devi prepared the breyani, and Goondie and
Jean Sully the turkey, and the ham and the salads.
Dots prepared the apple tart and Guin the fruit salad.

Janie Malherbe brought home-made buttered bread. And there were represented also all the nations under our sun. The Archbishop proposed the toast to me, but first he spoke about you, how you had sat in the chair by the door, receiving all your guests with your warm smile, so brave, so ill, so generous in your hospitality. Then he treated me to a very subdued kind of banter. I began seriously too, and said that I was remembering these things also; I reminded them that Edgar Brookes had said the year before, with a liberty that is permissible on such occasions, that I was the bravest man in South Africa and you were the bravest woman. And when I replied I ignored both compliments, but ever since had regretted that I ignored the second. Then I told our guests that on the day before Christmas I had met the Archbishop in the bottle store and had said to him, *Your Grace, I am surprised to see you here.* He countered that by saying, *one meets a lot of surprising people in bottle stores.* He then said to me, *do you know I've been at it since nine o'clock this morning?* And I replied, *Your Grace,* we *don't begin till sundown.* When I remarked to Murray Dell that the Archbishop had been subdued, he said to me, *quite rightly, it was you who had to tell us we could laugh again.*

After a little more banter, I asked the ladies to go to the dining-room, and Gatsha Buthelezi called out, *does that apply to the Zulus?* and I replied, *if any Zulu man feels that he should precede the womenfolk, he can go right now.* After that we all had a perfect supper. At 10.0 p.m. people started to leave, and at 11.0 p.m. only the family was left, and Pat and Sakuntala.

Janie, who brought the gift of bread, wrote to me the next day, *though Dorrie was not there in the flesh, one clearly felt aware of her sweet warm presence.*

Not sorrow or pain, neither sighing, but life everlasting.

19

Last night I suddenly remembered something that I had not thought of for forty years. It was the first intimation of your moral strength, for up till then you had been seeking it from me.

In October or November of 1925 your husband's sister in England decided to come out to see you, perhaps to comfort you. This must have posed some painful problems to you. Some other woman might have asked me to banish myself for a time, but you did not. You said to me that what had happened, had happened, and you could not hide or pretend. I think we agreed, easily and naturally, that although we would not hide our love, we would not parade it, and that you would have to give a good deal of time to your sister-in-law.

When she came, I was introduced to her, and as far as I remember, there was no coldness. But if I remember rightly, she decided to return to England sooner than she had meant to do.

I was to learn later that there was no pretence in you, no deceitfulness. What fortune that is, to fall in love with a woman knowing nothing of her except that she is alive and mischievous, and then to find this great integrity. Or perhaps one senses the existence of qualities before they have been manifested. Perhaps the eye is indeed the window of the soul, and your eyes were clear and teasing and unafraid.

20

They are all gone, and the house is desolate again. Nancy and Margaret spent the day going through all your possessions, and setting some aside as gifts for your friends. I myself shall keep your wedding ring. One treasure was discovered, the picture of the opening of our musical *Mkhumbane* in the Durban City Hall. There are the Shepstones, you and me, Hansi Pollak and Archbishop Hurley. We are all in black except you. You are wearing a magnificent white floral dress and a white stole and long white gloves. Your face is smiling, proud, serene and happy. You look beautiful.

Did I tell you that? Or do I only tell you now when you are no longer here to hear it? There are many things I wish I had told you. My advice to all young husbands and wives, and indeed to all husbands and wives, is not to be too niggardly with their words. You may well have said to me on the morning after *Mkhumbane*, holding out the newspaper with that embarrassed, defiant, pleased look that you had on such occasions, *what do you think of that?* And I might have said, *it's very good, especially of you.* But what I should have done was to go to you and hug you, and say, *you look beautiful*. You were not what one would call a beautiful woman; what made you look beautiful was that proud eager soul that looked out of the window of your eyes, proud partly because you were dressed like a queen, partly because of that miserable wretch your husband.

That was a night to remember, coming so soon after Sharpeville, with black men and women marching through the streets of Durban and Cape Town, and white men and women filled with anxiety and fear, and everyone conscious of colour and race, and there we sat in the City Hall, Indian people and Coloured people and African people and white people, listening to the first musical play presented by African actors, a play made by white and black hands. There was no fear in that hall. And to think that it has all come to an end, because our rulers decided it was unnatural and undesirable and repugnant to the traditions of our country, whatever they may be! To think that the way you lived your life was unnatural and undesirable!

21

When did your father and mother and Rad come back from England? I cannot remember. Let us say, November 1925. Whether you had written about me to your mother and Rad I do not know. I would guess that your mother was overjoyed, not so much to have me for a son-in-law, as to have you loved again. Mind you,

I wasn't a wholly poor acquisition, a young teacher who threw himself life and soul into the work of the school, was thought well of by his headmaster, liked by his pupils, and had that guileless look in his eyes!

Your mother kissed me and said, *you must be good to her*, and I know she was thinking of your marriage, so long delayed and then so brief. I said to her *I'll try to be that*. What Rad said to me, I cannot remember. Ruth was very shy, and you said to her in a mock dictatorial way, *kiss him, go on, kiss him*. Garry who was eleven and a kind of Huckleberry Finn, mumbled something to me that I couldn't hear. Your older brother Aubrey was also let into the secret and he congratulated me; indeed the only one who was told nothing was your father. Just why, I cannot remember. Was it thought that he would tell everybody? That would have been bad because in those days one had to mourn or pretend to mourn for a year. He was a strange man, and would wander from house to office, and from office to the village, and from the village back to the house and the office. He was a lawyer, but as far as I remember he seldom appeared in court. If one met him on one of these journeys he would grunt or mumble something and pass on. I never saw him embrace your mother, or any of you, though I have no doubt he did so when it was brought to his notice that someone was going away to school or to Durban or to London. He must have noticed that I was more and more at Morningview, but I don't know how long it took him to find out what I was doing there. Even then he said nothing, and continued to say nothing until the day I asked him if I could marry you. What he then grunted or mumbled I cannot remember, but he could well have said, *have you asked Mother?* It was she in fact who was the head of the family, except in matters of money, and in those even she was a little afraid of him. You were all afraid of him about money. For him to give money was as painful as if he had had to agree to let an organ be torn out of his body. It was always your mother who had to go to him to ask for money, and he would bellow like a bull that has been wounded.

Your mother was a remarkable woman, much more austere and forbidding than any of her children. I admired and respected her, but I behaved towards her respectfully rather than lovingly, and I think she was hurt by this. How could I do other than respect her, who had imparted such a love of uprightness to her children? Her force of character was far greater than that of your father, and she treated him with a humorous tolerance of his grunting and mumbling and bellowing. Sometimes she would get under his guard, and he would break out into a sudden unwilling smile that transformed his face. It was she who spent her time with the children. He spent little, and this little was made less because he went to bed almost immediately after dinner. He used to rise with the roosters, though what he did, I do not know. One habit he had of which your mother was tolerant though it annoyed her at times, and that was to go into the kitchen and throw oddments of spices and chillies and curry into the pots and pans on the stove.

It was into this family that I was now admitted, and it filled me with joy and pride. Just as I adopted your

·–[37]–·

country, so did I adopt your family. One other thing happened too. You gladdened your mother's heart by going back to worship and communion. And I write here that despite all our faults and sins, our love of Christ and the good stayed with us all our lives, and took us both into deep waters.

22

Your grandmother's family was also remarkable. Your grandfather Robert Gold and his wife Jane emigrated to South Africa from Eskdale, on the east coast of Scotland, in 1860. They were given a farm at Highflats, in that same beautiful and virgin countryside, though less hilly than in the environs of Ixopo. This farm they called Eskdale also, and there Robert Gold and his wife brought up a family of ten sons and four daughters, of which the eldest daughter was your mother Agnes.

They could have come to no place more beautiful or suitable; the rain and the mist, the grass and the bracken, and the forlorn crying of birds, could have come out of the pages of Lewis Grassic Gibbon. The tales of their exploits were legion, reminding one of the tales of the Herries. They were called the Maguzas, a name which derives (I assume, but nobody knows) from the Zulu word *Amaguza*, meaning snuffboxes, though again I do not know why this should be so. The Maguzas were renowned and formidable, and were regarded with a mixture of awe and wonder and amusement.

I was received hospitably into this wild family, which still retained much of the rough-and-readiness of the farming pioneers. Of course I was only a schoolmaster, but was not Grannie Gold's brother, R. D. Clark, a schoolmaster too, the famous headmaster of Maritzburg College, and had he not left to the school a library with so many books that you could have dropped one per yard on the road from Eskdale to Highflats, and still have some over? And this same R. D. Clark, was he not M.A. Oxon, which means M.A. Oxford of course, so that no one should be thinking that Grannie Gold came from an ignorant bunch of people? There was a story told of herself and Jack Arnott. Jack Arnott was also a pioneer, who had set up a butcher's shop at Highflats. Later, when he became a man of substance and a General during the war of 1914–18, and had a fine farm of his own, and was held in great respect, he had an argument with Grannie Gold, who clinched it by saying to him, *I'd have you remember-r, young Arr-nott, that you were only a butcher-r's boy*.

When the Golds and their relatives-in-law gathered together, there was always a call for tales of the Maguzas, and the Maguzas themselves would call out, *Doris, come Doris, where's Doris?* And if you did not come immediately, they would call out, *come Doris, a story of yon Maguzas*. Meanwhile your mother's face would be one unending beam, and your father's would wear a half-proud, half-embarrassed smile, to have a daughter in such demand. Then there would be loud clapping, and you would emerge from the passage, complete with bonnet and plaid and kilt and sporran and stockings and all, and that cocky and confident smile on your face, and your head tilted back, and a look which said plainly, and quite immodestly, *Maguzas, you haven't seen entertainment until tonight.* And one of the first stories you told, which always brought that house down, was the story of Kathy Farrer who screwed up her courage to borrow ten shillings from her old and deaf and avaricious Auntie Jock of Flosh House, and of how, when Kathy was slow in paying back the money, Auntie Jock would call out at her, especially if visitors were present, *Do you mind the pound I lent you, Kathy?* And of course if one knew the identity of Kathy and the aunt, one would laugh one's head off.

There was another story of the time when Henry Gold, the fourth of Grannie Gold's children, shot some pellets into the legs of an African trespasser, which to tell the truth, in those pioneering days was an offence not gravely regarded by the pioneers. However, the magistrate took another view, and fined Henry a certain amount of money. Henry was not one to take this lying down, this whittling away of the privileges of pioneers. He, who himself kept polo ponies of good parentage, bought a broken-down horse from one of his labourers, called it Magistrate, and entered it in the main race of the forthcoming gymkhana to be held at Himeville (or perhaps Underberg). Then when the leading horses were thundering down to the winning post, Henry went out in great anger to vituperate against the luckless Magistrate. *Come on Magistrate,* he shouted, *You damn fool Magistrate. Is that all you can do Magistrate? Ach, to hell with you Magistrate.*

What the magistrate thought of this, is not part of the story. What the Maguzas thought of it, is part of mine. They laughed, they cried, their eyes ran with tears, they coughed, they spluttered, but whatever they did, they thought that Doris was one of the greatest performers of all time. And who knows? Perhaps you were.

And one story more. In the Maguza family there was bound to be some quarrelling, and Henry and Donald had not spoken to each other for some time, so that it was an occasion for rejoicing when they decided to be reconciled, and Donald came up from the city to his brother's farm 'Dartford', near Underberg. After dinner they decided to play bridge, which was a family failing of the Maguzas. What is more, Donald, whether by cutting the cards, or because it was part of the reconciliation, found himself paired with Henry, and to play with Henry required certain saintly qualities which Donald did not possess in great abundance. The end of the game was violent, presumably some disagreement on the calling or the play. Donald growled, *I'll not stay another moment in this damned house*, to which Henry replied, as befitted a host, *I'll take you to Underberg station.* Now the road from Dartford to Underberg was in the main a descending road, and was made of earth, and when it rained, the water was carried from one side of the road to the other by diagonal drains, and then into the grass of the veld. One could not drive too fast on such a road, because the rear portion of the car would buck each time a drain was crossed. What is more, the cars of those days had canvas roofs or hoods, and this hood was supported by wooden slats or bars. Therefore it was possible for a

·–[41]–·

driver to cross these drains in such a way that a passenger in the rear seat would be thrown up against the supporting bar, and be killed or perhaps merely injured.

This is now exactly what Henry did, and it is exactly what happened to Donald. When it had happened, one supposes, at least twice, Donald could endure it no longer, and he shouted at Henry, *put me down, I'll walk.* Then Henry, as befitted a host, said, *I'll take your bags to the station.* So Donald was left on the road, and Henry drove on to Underberg and deposited the bags on the station platform, where in those days they could have stayed indefinitely. On the way back Henry passed his brother on the road, and as befitted a host, waved him goodbye, but his guest did not respond.

I myself saw one of these reconciliations, and that was at Morningview after your mother's funeral in 1931. This time the pair to be reconciled were again Henry and Donald, and your brother Aubrey took charge of the reconciling. He drew two chalk lines, one at each end of the long Morningview veranda (you remember, where you first pressed against me?) and then with great precision a third, halfway between the two. Henry and Donald were to start simultaneously, and to reach the middle line simultaneously, where they were to shake hands, this action to signify a declaration of everlasting peace. Alas, Henry thought that Donald was not walking fast enough, and when he felt convinced of it, he left the course with a snort of anger, leaving Donald no one with whom to be reconciled.

Where are you now, mischievous and impudent mocker of the Maguzas, with a mockery that could make them laugh because it had no malice in it? Does anyone ever mock them now, and bring down the house with the question, *do you mind the pound I lent you Kathy?* Where is that look of mischief now? For it was part of a miracle formèd of the dust, and now that the miracle has returned to dust, has it gone for ever? Or is it, as it should be, a very part of heaven?

23

I shall write down quickly something that happened to me this afternoon. Nancy and Margaret had set aside your brown overcoat and a red hat for Elizabeth, and I took them to her. She was overwhelmed and broke out into a torrent of English and Afrikaans, revealing a depth of emotion that I had not expected. And again that thing rose in my throat and I dared not speak to her. I went to the car and she followed me, still pouring out her gratitude, and still I dared not speak to her. I waved to her and drove back to the desolate house.

24

In what month I took you to see my father and mother and sisters and brother, I cannot now remember. But

I can well remember our home, so different from yours. My parents were Christadelphians, they disapproved of the pomp and panoply of churches, their own religious practices were the essence of simplicity. The churches they disapproved of most were the Anglican and the Roman Catholic. My father smoked but not my mother, and this differentiation enjoyed almost the status of an article of faith. The theatre was wicked, but not the cinema! I never saw alcohol in our home, though I remember my father — and perhaps my mother — taking a little wine in a neighbour's home. On Sundays we went to the 'meeting' and the only recreation permitted was walking. We were seldom allowed out of the house except when we went to school or on an errand, and our friends were either chosen by or approved of by my father. He was a stern and sometimes a cruel man, and though I have no doubt that he loved us, he was seldom able to demonstrate it. My mother was tender and loving, quite subservient to my father, despite the fact that she herself was a person of strong and noble character. I record one other thing also, that it was in this stern home that we learned to love and cherish the good, but I must also record that this loving and cherishing of the good was inseparably bound up with a rigid code of beliefs that I later rejected when I found that others loved and cherished the good with codes of beliefs quite other than the one I had been taught was indispensable to salvation.

It was into this home that I had to take you, a widow of a few months, a woman nearly six years older than myself, a woman who smoked and did not eschew

·–[44]–·

alcohol and did not believe in any puritanical observ-
ance of Sundays, and to cap it all, an Anglican, a
member of that popish church that was worldly and
pretended to be spiritual, whose ministers were called
priests and wore outlandish garments, a church where
Sunday by Sunday one gabbled the same rigmarole.
I did not take any of these matters lightly, but the one
that troubled me most was my father's utter and
irrational condemnation of women who smoked. I
pleaded with you to stop it, but you would not. I venture to think (and I venture to think I am right in so
venturing) that you and Rad regarded yourselves as
pioneers in this form of emancipation of women. In the
end you agreed that you would not smoke in front of
my father and mother and sisters. In front of my
brother Atholl it did not matter, for with a cool and
impudent candour that I did not possess he had thrown
over everything in my parents' teaching with which
he had no patience. He was also a pioneer in emancipation, for he called my mother Eunice and my grandmother Lisbeth, or Elspeth or Bessie; he used to advise
and admonish them in a way that was inimitably his
own. You and he were soon friends, for you were both
mischievous. I think that my mother loved you instant-
ly, in spite of all the obstacles I have written of above
(except the smoking, of which she knew nothing). And
I think my sisters did too (Dorrie was ten and Ailsa
twelve years younger than you), and I know that this
love grew with the years. My father you didnt' take
to, and I don't blame you; to your family you called
him 'Jimmy' and he must have been quite baffled to
know what to make of you; you were not the kind

of woman known to his circumscribed world.

I myself had never become a Christadelphian, largely because my mind would not consent to any rigid code of belief, and I hurt my mother by saying to her that I judged a person by his life and deeds, not by his beliefs. In Ixopo I went to the Methodist church, this being the first step away from sectarianism. But already in my mind – unknown to you – I was preparing to enter your popish church, with its outlandish garments and its repetitious rigmarole. One of the reasons was you, of course, but the other was that Anglicanism, in the words about you that Norman wrote from prison, did not deny the bad so much as it affirmed the good.

I must add one thing. I asked you to give up smoking for the wrong reason. I asked you to do it for my own comfort and convenience. I should have asked you for quite another reason, that it would destroy your lungs, and cause you to end your life in continuous distress, and cause that terrible rhythm, of a box rising, staying up a moment, then falling with a bang till it rose again, a spasm that made the heart of the watcher fit to break.

But alas, I did not know that reason then.

25

In the middle of December 1925 I went back to my parents' home for Christmas. So far as I know, I then received my first letters from you. They were addressed to 'My Dearest One'. I cannot describe the joy, the pride, in being so called. After all, there was your mother, there was your father (I realized that he was not a contender), Rad, Ruth and Garry. I doubt if I saw you during that long Christmas holiday of six weeks, which in its way was an extraordinary thing. Then the great day came when I would return to Ixopo, and go to Morningview, and be welcomed and loved by you. The anticipation of it I cannot describe, for it was quite indescribable. Of all the joys of my life, the joy of reunion with you after separation was the greatest. And when I write about the joy of reunion, I mean as much as I mean anything, the joy of physical reunion.

I find it almost impossible to believe that you did not know at what time I would arrive. When I reached Morningview your mother and Rad and Ruth all came to greet me. But you, the expected one, I did not see. You were in the bath, they said. We sat in what was called the drawing-room in those days, and they all talked to me, but how could I talk to them? I seem to remember that in the end they left me to sit there by myself. How long did I sit there? It would be wrong to try now to remember. Ten minutes I could have forgiven, but it was more like thirty. After some time your mother came to say, *she won't be long now.* I seem to remember that she looked unhappy, whether for me or for you or for her hopes for your happiness, I cannot say. Were there comings and goings? Did they go to you and plead with you and tell you that such a thing could not be done? I do not know. All I know was the hurt of waiting for a lover who did not come, or who would not come, or who was afraid to come, to meet her dearest one.

Well eventually you came. That is obvious, for otherwise I would not be writing this. How did we embrace? Was it with constraint? Alas for Memory, she will not help me at all. You must have seen the hurt on my face, you must have expected it to be there.

Why had I not already walked out of the house before you came out of your interminable bath? Why didn't I say to your mother, using cold words, *If I am wanted, if any person should happen to want me, I can be found at the boys' hostel.* But I could not. I did not know such words, I was in love, I was twenty-three. If I had been thirty-three I might have walked out and never come back, and there would not have been any David and Jonathan, or their lovely wives, or their lovely children that have so comforted me. I might have married some other girl, some girl perhaps who would have been afraid to go with me along dangerous roads, and would have given me craven sons and daughters, and craven daughters- and sons-in-law. But I did not, because I was in love. And why I stayed in love, God only knows.

So you told me why you had kept me waiting. You had gone to Jean, a widow herself, whom you thought to be a woman of great wisdom. You went to her because you had begun to doubt the depth of your love for me. And she had told you that you had been caught on the rebound, and that your love must be suspect because you had been lonely and had wanted to be loved again, and there in Ixopo there was no man of your age or older who was available to love you; therefore in your loneliness you turned to a young eager boy, whom you liked certainly, and you played tennis with him and exchanged banter with him, and even took him down a peg or two on All Fools' Day.

Perhaps she told you — I do not know — that you must not be impatient to be loved, you must bide your time, you must go out into the world and see people and things, you were still young and attractive, and you would certainly marry again, and this blunder would be forgotten. Perhaps she told you out of her wisdom that I was young too, and I would get over it and marry some sweet young girl who would love me better than you could ever do.

And then, either you told me that you yourself thought it would be wiser for me to marry some younger woman, or you asked me, *don't you think you ought to marry some younger woman?* And I said to you in spite of my pain, *I don't want to marry some other woman.*

I do not profess to understand why after all these years of your warmth and your comradeship, I should feel again the pain of that long gone time. I would be nobler, wouldn't I, if I didn't feel it? But then I would not be myself, nor would I be writing what I am. For I am writing a story of love which began with joy and pain, and ended in steadfastness. I write it because I am compelled to write it. I do not come into this room and stare at the paper as I have done so many times before. I am eager to begin, and if I am called away,

I am impatient to return. And it shall all be there, the joy and the pain and the steadfastness. Some people will say that you wouldn't have liked it, but I think you would have looked at me in your brave serious way and you would have said, *if you feel it should be written that way, then write it that way*. And this is how I feel it should be written.

26

It was the first time that I was ever angry with you, for taking our affairs to a woman who was almost a stranger to me, who had a worldly wisdom no doubt, but no spiritual understanding that I had ever discerned. Once angry thoughts start running, they run in packs, snarling and snapping and biting. Who asked me so often to your parents' house? And who arranged for me to coach your sister? And who suggested that my hands should be read? Could you not see that I was in love? Why did you not go to Jean then and tell her what was happening to you, and ask her what you should do about it? Why first bear me up in your arms to a great height, and then take your arms away?

What happened then? Did someone come and say, *it's time for dinner*? What do you speak about at dinner when your lover has just told you that perhaps you should find another?

After dinner you and I went out into the garden with a rug and cushions. Did we talk first, or embrace and caress each other? I cannot remember. All that

I can remember is that I said again that I did not want to marry some other person, I wanted to marry you. You told me that you had not ceased to care for me, you had rather decided that you did not care for me enough or that you could not care for me enough, not as much as I deserved. Then we decided that we would not part from one another, and you hoped that the day would come when you would love me as I deserved. Just how we formulated all this is another of those things that I cannot remember.

At that age I could hardly comprehend your situation, but now I think I do. I think your sense of guilt was twofold, first, because you had loved so soon after your husband's death, second because you had encouraged to love you a boy six years younger than yourself, to whom you could never give the raptures of first love. I think you thought a great deal in the categories of first love and other love, because that was a romantic tradition of those days. I would not say it exists no longer, but it has today nothing like the hold it once had.

The irony of the whole affair is that I would never have thought your love defective if you had not told me that it was. And whether I was also to blame, whether I was jealous or too possessive or too demanding, I cannot remember. But I am willing to believe that this was so.

Let me write one more thing. Although I remember these things with pain, I did not live in pain. I was in love with life and with school and with its boys and girls, I was in love with the hills and the valleys of the Ixopo countryside, I was in love with you. And

there was the hope — held out by you — that one day
whatever was lacking in your love would be repaired.

27

C. S. Lewis opens 'A Grief Observed' with these
words:

> No one ever told me that grief is so like fear. I
> am not afraid, but the sensation is like being
> afraid.

This is not altogether my experience. Yesterday and
today are the first days that I have felt afraid. I am
afraid of living without you. I am afraid I shall never
want to do anything any more. I wrote earlier that I
did not wish to live in the past, but now that is what
I am afraid of doing. This happened to me yesterday,
and again today.

I know it is wrong. In my language, it is a sin that
I am committing, against God who gave me life and
gifts so that I might use them, against you whose life
was lived in the present, and against my neighbour
who might have need of me. This sin that I am
committing, if I persist in it, will corrupt my remembrance of you, and make it resentful and self-pitying
rather than thankful and joyful.

Did I do right this morning? I prayed to you, you,
wherever you are, and in whatever condition you may
be, that you should regard me with love and mercy,

and intercede for me so that I can come out of this valley of darkness. And I fear that I am not supposed by canonical law or whatever law it may be, to pray to you.

Where are you, my love? And in what condition? That your body has returned to the dust, that I know. But what has happened to you, to your love and your warmth and your courage? Your dust is indestructible, but you, you yourself, were you also indestructible? Did you, you yourself, have no being apart from that body that has returned to the dust?

I write these words with great care. I have no desire to believe something just because I desire to believe it. The Archbishop said,

With the passing of Dorrie the visible fellowship is broken; but death does not put an end to real fellowship; prayer goes on and love continues — from the land of the living, from the joy of Paradise, whence all pain and grief have fled away, where the light of Christ's countenance ever shines.

Was he speaking about Heaven? Are you in Heaven? Are you re-united there to your first husband, your father and your mother, your much-loved sister Rad, your brother Ray who died as a boy, the one you said I would have liked especially, because we were so like each other? Would your first husband perhaps not be there, because he was not a believer, and would I perhaps go there because I am a believer? This whole speculation is to me so grotesque that I cannot indulge in it. If I wish to touch you again, if I wish again to feel your warm and loving body pressed against mine after long separation, then I can do it only in memory.

I do not ask or expect that one day I shall hold you again in my arms.

Did Vachel Lindsay believe there was such a place when he wrote his great poem 'General William Booth enters into Heaven'? When I am asked to give public readings, I dare not read that poem, because although I could manage the first six stanzas with their almost mocking description of the blind general leading his blaring band round the courts of heaven, apparently without so much as a by-your-leave, I cannot trust myself to read aloud the last stanza, which suddenly reveals that this apparently mocking poem is a thing as deep as anything in literature.

> And when Booth halted by the curb for prayer
> He saw his Master thro' the flag-filled air.
> Christ came gently with a robe and crown
> For Booth the soldier, while the crowd knelt down.
> He saw King Jesus. They were face to face,
> And he knelt a-weeping in that holy place.
> Are you washed in the blood of the Lamb?

Vachel Lindsay is saying something to me to which my whole being responds. My mind does not stand sceptically on the side-lines, watching my emotions making fools of themselves; it is my whole self which is there. But only a poet or a saint can say that kind of thing to us. Once heaven is made a matter of fact, it becomes ludicrous.

Here again I go, as I so often do, to Francis of Assisi. There was not a thought in his mind that his death meant the end of his relationship with his friend and his most High Lord. On the contrary it would continue, and it would continue for ever. When the doctor told him he was soon to die, he stretched out his hands and cried aloud with joy, 'Welcome, Sister Death.' Then he added to his 'Canticle of the Sun' the stanza:

Praised be my Lord for our sister, the bodily death,
From which no living man can flee.
Woe to them who die in mortal sin,
Blessed those who shall find themselves in
  Thy most holy will,
For the second death shall do them no ill.

Francis wrote of the 'second death' because he had died the first time on the day when he came down from his horse to kiss the leper on the Umbrian plain. It was on that day that he entered into eternal life. It was on that day that he found himself in God's will, and it is in that will that he died. And being in that will, he still *is*.

This belief, and the possibility of holding it, depend of course entirely on the primary belief that God is the Creator of Heaven and Earth, and that we can be the instruments of His peace, and thereby ourselves become part of the divine creativity. God is He within whom we move and have our being. He holds us, and indeed the universe, in His will, which is eternal.

Not long before you died I wrote this prayer:

Lord, give me grace to die in Thy will.
Prepare me for whatever place or condition awaits me.
Let me die true to those things I believe to be true,
And suffer me not through any fear of death to fall from
  Thee.

Lord, give me grace to live in Thy will also.
Help me to master any fear, any desire, that prevents
me from living in Thy will. Make me, O Lord, the
 instrument
of Thy peace, that I may know eternal life.
Into Thy hands I commend my spirit.

I believe you died in God's will, and that you are
eternal, but of your place and condition I know nothing,
and I do not speculate about it. I remember those last
communions, when you lay back so childlike and
humble, and received the bread and the wine. At those
last communions you were at times with us, and at
times not. At your last communion, on Wednesday
October 18th, you were dozing when it was time to
receive the bread, and Murray put it into my hand,
and I placed it in your mouth. Then it fell out and I
had to put it back again. Then he put the small chalice
into my hand, and I gave you the wine and kissed
you. And all of us knew, Murray and David and
Jonathan and Elizabeth and I, that you would never
receive them again.

If I am ever in any kind of sense of the word to *know*
you again, there will be no jealousies and angers and
arrogances and impatiences, but only joy. And sorrow
and pain shall be no more, neither sighing, but life
everlasting.

And if such things are never to be, then I give
thanks this day for what is and has been. And I can
doubly give thanks, for during the writing of these
words, I have come out of the valley of darkness.

Did you intercede for me?

28

When lilacs last in the dooryard bloom'd,
And the great star early drooped in the western
    sky in the night,
I mourn'd, and yet shall mourn with ever-
    returning spring.

These lines have been haunting me for days, and I did not know why at first. Then suddenly I knew. It is because the tibouchinas, the mauve and the pink, are bursting into bloom, and the Zanzibar balsams at the gate are magnificent, a glorious bed of white and pink and salmon and red. The last time they bloomed you were in King George V Hospital, not knowing that your life was coming to its end. Some days you were ill and in great distress, and other days you were bright and eager like that girl on the tennis-court, so full of hope, so eager to get home again, so eager to have a real bath again, so eager to wean yourself from the oxygen from which you could never be weaned.

Each time that I went to the hospital and each time that I returned home, if it were still light, I would see the tibouchinas. So now, when I see them again, they speak to me of you. I see you too, in your hospital bed, with your eager face and your determined voice, and I hear you say to me, *I am going to get well, and I am going home, and I am going to get into the bath —you must help me, Alan — I want to feel the water on my body, you don't know what it means to me to feel the water on my body.*

Yes. I know what it means to you, my love. And I see your eager face, and I wish my face could be eager too, and I wish I could say to you, *Yes, you're coming home, and you're going to get into the bath — yes, I'll be helping you — and you're going to feel the water on your body again.* But I can't do it. There's no eagerness in me, only grief. When I say good night to you, I say, *sleep well, my sweet,* and it surprises me, for never before in my life did I call you *my sweet*.

I wanted to write a letter to you, to thank you for the blessings of our common life, and for your courage and gaiety and zest, and for your contempt of cruelty and cant, and for your belief that man is not born to go down on his belly before the State, and for your crossnesses when we were playing games, and your unfailing rising to the bait when we were teasing you. But they wouldn't let me write it, because you would ask, *why do you write such a letter? Is it because you think I am going to die?* No, they wanted you to go on hoping these empty hopes.

And I think they were right, for you were afraid of dying and of death, and had been ever since I knew you. You never liked me to say, *when I pop off, you'll be able to do what you like, pick all the flowers in the garden, and not have books lying about the house.* You would say, *please Alan, don't joke about it.* So I did not write any letter.

Yet I was distressed to think that we could not talk about the culminating event of our married life. Once when you were in King George V you said to Murray Dell, *I think I'm coming to the end of the road.* You never said to him, or to me, *am I coming to the end of the road?* If you had asked me, I wanted to be able to put my arms around you, and to say, *yes, my love.* But they all said *No.*

There is one thing for which I can be thankful. When Aubrey Burns, the first person ever to read *Cry, the Beloved Country*, in his house in California through which those four redwood trees were growing — when he came at last to visit us he wanted of course to see Ixopo and Carisbrooke and the hills that are lovely beyond any singing of it. When we had seen it all, I took him into the church where you and I were married, on July 2nd, 1928, and there I knelt and gave thanks for our married life. That evening he and I went to visit you at King George V and I told you what I had done, and your whole face lit up with joy. So you were told it after all.

There is another thing that I remember, one night at King George V when your old gaiety suddenly returned. I was saying good night to you, and you said to me in Afrikaans, as mischievous as ever you were, *slaap lekker, slaap alleen.**

And yet another thing. When you came home at long last, some night in June or July, you suddenly said to me, *you're not a bad old stick.* When you were well, you were warm and smiling. Dr H. said to me, *your wife is a wonderful woman.* And I said to him gravely, *that is true.*

These are the lights along a dark and sorrowful road; and by the grace of God, it is the lights that one remembers.

* Sleep well, sleep alone.

You told me you cared for me, but you did not care for me enough, though you hoped that one day you would care for me enough. And I accepting it, we did not part. Why I accepted it, I cannot now explain. I think there was at least one reason. I was in love with my work as much as I was in love with you. I was ambitious and wanted to rise to the top of my profession. I think it is right that a man should love his vocation as much as he loves his bride.

Although my university degree was in Mathematics and Physics, and although I had never taken Chemistry beyond the high school, yet I found that I had to teach what was known as Physical Science, a subject half Physics and half Chemistry. I should have told my headmaster, Wilfred Buss, that I was not qualified to teach Physical Science. Perhaps I did, perhaps I did not. Perhaps I had already found a treasure on the tennis-court and did not want to leave Ixopo. I do not know.

One of the experiments which a chemistry teacher has to perform is to demonstrate that the element sodium has the power to break up water into its constituent elements, hydrogen and oxygen, and to form caustic soda and free hydrogen. Sodium is kept in paraffin to prevent it from oxidizing. But our small piece of sodium in the Ixopo High School laboratory refused to perform. I cut piece after piece from it, but it refused to react with water. Where it came from, I do not know, but apparently its external surfaces were heavily oxidized. Finally in desperation I took it and the Physical Science class into the recreation ground of the school. I made them stand back and then with a pipette I dropped water on the remaining piece of sodium. Suddenly it went off with a tremendous explosion, blinding and searing me, presumably the caustic soda and the burning hydrogen together. Wilfred Buss rushed me in his car to the district surgeon, who applied some soothing ointment to my eyes, and ordered that I be taken to Pietermaritzburg at once, in the hope of saving my sight.

The news was all over the village in a few minutes. I, blinded and bandaged and now free of the unendurable pain, waited passively for whatever might be done for me. Who came to Pietermaritzburg beside Wilfred Buss and myself, I do not remember, except for one. You came and sat by me in the car, and held me protectively and lovingly, and you whispered to me, *I haven't any doubts any more.*

30

I am here in Nigel, and am staying with Ruth, and we have been recalling one of the things that so endeared you to your family, and that was the way you got so angry when playing cards. Our favourite game was 'reformatory bridge', which was based on a game called 'Haul', but ours we thought was better. If there were four players, each received thirteen cards, and the dealer might say, *I call five hearts.* That meant that any player taking five tricks in hearts added five points to his score, but any player taking less or more diminished his score by the number by which he had fallen short or exceeded the number five. We all started with twenty points to avoid scoring in minuses.

Sometimes you would get a good hand, and you might say, *I call seven clubs*. In such a case each of the other players would try to take no tricks at all, unless of course one of them thought he might make the seven himself. How furious you would be if you led the ace of clubs, and one of the others, having no clubs, threw away the ace of diamonds on it, and how much greater your fury would be if that player was myself.

You would say, *Alan, you are the meanest dirtiest player I have ever met*. Perhaps you would switch to diamonds immediately, and play the four, and David would play the three and Jonathan the two, and I, having no more diamonds, would throw away the ace of spades. By this time your fury knew no bounds. You might throw down your cards and say, *I refuse to play*, and your face would be wearing a sulky look, and how much of it was real and how much was not, was something we could never be sure about. You might say to me, *everyone thinks you are generous, but only we know just how mean you are*. Then Jonathan might say, *But, Mrs P., in this game one plays to be mean*, and you would reply, accenting every word, *one does not play to be mean, one plays to have a happy evening*. And then I might say, *that is exactly what we are not doing*. The impudence of this remark, and its coming from such a source, would rekindle your passion, and you would say, *And why? And why are we not having a happy*

·–[62]–·

evening? Because of your dirty play. Then the gale would suddenly blow itself out, and you would pick up the cards defiantly, and play another, as though challenging us to commit any further act of meanness. The sulky look would go, and if you were feeling generous, you would favour us with a half-willing, half-unwilling smile.

Sometimes Ruth and Dick would be staying with us, and if you put up one of these exhibitions, Ruth would look at you with a mixture of amusement, because it was funny, and affectionate sympathy, because you were her much-loved sister, and apprehension, because of the uncertainty as to how much of it was real and how much was not. As for Dick, who never experienced such exhibitions at home, he would laugh his head off, and at the same time be filled with admiration that such a blend of love and denunciation could exist at all.

I would imagine that this happened once out of every three or four times we played. Sometimes we would bring it on, by some complacent or boasting remark about our skill and strategy, but at other times, if your luck was really shocking, we would all keep silent, knowing that there was thunder in the air. Then suddenly the storm would break over our innocent and not altogether unwilling heads. You had proved true to form after all.

I do not remember that a game ever ended in anger. The thunder would boom and the lightning crackle and the rain come down, but at bedtime the stars were out in the sky. And not one of us would have had you any different.

·– [63] –·

In a way you were only maintaining the family tradition. For we would remind you – if it were safe – that once your Grannie Gold, sitting by the fireside at Eskdale, playing bridge and losing, suddenly swept up all the cards and threw them into the fire.

31

It has suddenly occurred to me that we have not played our game of reformatory bridge since you died. This is not out of respect for your memory. It is because some irreplaceable spice has gone out of the game. Not one of us can produce that same blend of denunciation and love. Not one of us stands in the some relation to the others as we stood in relation to you.

32

I did not lose my sight after all. The final damage was a defective tear-duct in the right eye, but Dr I. in Pietermaritzburg made me a new one which has served me well for forty-two years. When I came out of hospital you took me down to Scottburgh, still protective and loving. On September 20th, 1926, we became officially engaged. It was exactly one year since you had found it so uncomfortable, first sitting in your chair, and then sitting on the floor in front of the fire.

The halcyon days had returned. Partnering you in

the second Ixopo tennis team, playing matches at High-flats, Umzimkulu, Lufafa Road, Eastwolds, all of them places set in that wonderful countryside of hills and farms and grass and bracken. Buying a motor car together, a Chevrolet, second-hand for a hundred and seventy-five pounds (new then it cost two hundred and twenty-five pounds, today about fifteen hundred pounds). Achieving the perfect balance between duty and pleasure, willing to do almost any extra duty at school, supervising games and making gardens and going on expeditions into the hills, acting in your plays, all with an energy that was limitless.

Our first Matriculation examination (Standard X) was disastrous. We had four entrants and all failed. Your mother took Ruth away and sent her to Pietermaritzburg. The postmaster took his daughter away and sent her to Northern Natal. A third parent took his son away and sent him to Maritzburg College. The next year we had three entrants, and two passed in the third class. I might have thought I was not fitted for teaching, except that we did excellently in the Junior Certificate (Standard VIII) and gained our first first-class pass. The next year the results were still better in the Junior Certificate and much better in the Matriculation. Parents from other parts began to send us their sons and daughters. Your mother said to you, and you repeated it to me with pride, *Alan is going to make a mark in the world.* I heard this not without pride myself.

The more I knew your mother, the greater grew my respect for her. Her standards of conduct were high. but not puritanical. These standards she imparted to her family, not least yourself. It was as united a family as I have ever seen, and I was happy in being part of it.

All this was your mother's work, and I wish I could have loved her as much as I respected her. There is something in my nature, good or bad or neutral I do not know, that will not let me love a matriarch. Yet I never came into conflict with her will. I think both she and I knew that it would have been a disaster for us all.

I once played a joke on her. Your father had engaged a young clerk, Laurie F., whom I had taught at school, a quiet, serious, young lad of about eighteen. Your mother took a dislike to him, apparently because she thought he made himself too much at home. Now one of the proud possessions of your parents was a new Buick, the most luxurious car in the whole countryside. So I wrote the following note to your mother:

> Dear Mrs Francis,
>   I have to go home this week-end and would like to borrow the Buick.
>   Yours sincerely,
>   Laurie F——

I showed you and Rad the letter, and you arranged to have it delivered when the whole family was together just before dinner. The result was electrical. Your mother opened the letter and read it with a look of shocked incredulity. Her hands shook as she held it out. *The impudence of it*, she said, *the little upstart, the Buick!* You took it, and then Rad, and then Ruth, while your mother poured down imprecations on Laurie's innocent head. Then you and Rad joined in, *What impudence! What unbelievable cheek!* Your mother said, *I'll Buick him!* She realized that this was funny, and for a moment amusement struggled with anger on her face. Then the anger returned. She was clearly about to do something, so I thought it was time to tell her that it was not Laurie who had written the letter, but myself. The family was convulsed with laughter, and eventually she laughed too, saying to me, *Alan, you wretch!*

33

I rang Sister Elspeth the other afternoon and I reminded her that she had said that you would be interceding for me. I asked her what theological justification she had for such a statement, and when she said she did not know, I suggested she asked Reverend Mother. What came back to me was not an answer to my question at all, but one of the most remarkable prayers that I have ever read:

O God, the God of the spirits of all flesh, in Whose embrace all creatures live, in whatsoever world or condition they be: I beseech Thee for her whose name and dwelling-place and every need Thou knowest. Lord, vouchsafe her light and rest, peace and refreshment, joy and consolation in Paradise, in the companionship of saints, in the presence of Christ, in the ample folds of Thy great love.

Grant that her life may unfold itself in Thy sight, and find a sweet employment in the spacious fields of eternity. If she hath ever been hurt or maimed by any unhappy word or deed of mine, I pray Thee of Thy great pity to heal and restore her, that she may serve thee without hindrance.

Tell her, O gracious Lord, if it may be, how much I love her and miss her, and long to see her again; and, if there be ways in which she may come, vouchsafe her to me as a guide and guard, and grant me a sense of her nearness as Thy laws permit.

If in aught I can minister to her peace, be pleased of Thy love to let this be; and mercifully keep me from every act which may deprive me of the sight of her as soon as our trial-time is over, or mar the fullness of our joy when the end of the days hath come.

Pardon, O gracious Lord and Father, whatsoever is amiss in this my prayer, and let Thy will be done, for my will is blind and erring, but Thine is able to do exceeding abundantly above all that we ask or think; through Jesus Christ our Lord.

Amen.

This prayer is based on many tremendous assumptions. One is that the one departed is in God's embrace, in Paradise, in the presence of Christ and the companionship of the saints. A second is that she lives, and that her life is being lived to some purpose. A third is that God, *if it may be*, may tell her that she is loved and missed, and, *if there be ways*, may give her to the one who loves and misses her, as a guard and guide, and may allow her nearness to be felt *if His laws permit.* A fourth assumption is that she and the one who prays for her will be reunited, and the one who prays for her will *see* her, if he does nothing that may deprive him of such a fulfilment. Therefore the one who prays, aware no doubt of the magnitude of his assumptions, asks to be pardoned whatever is amiss in this his prayer.

Although I myself am aware of the magnitude of these assumptions, and although I believe that not one of them can be held except in faith, yet I can pray this prayer with all my being. My whole being responds to it as it responds to the vision of General Booth, who with his

> air of high command
> unabated in that holy land,

yet knelt a-weeping in that holy place. So do I respond to the prayer of Francis of Assisi, and to his cry of greeting to his Sister Death.

Therefore I shall pray this prayer for you with all my being. Never could I have made a prayer for myself so humble and so trusting. The petition that your life should find a sweet employment in the fields of eternity is very moving to me, and conjures up the picture of you at the typewriter, typing everything that I ever wrote, suggesting the changing of a word or the removing of some obscurity, saying to me sometimes, *It's very good,* saying to me even, *I couldn't have written it better myself.*

If she has ever been hurt or maimed by any unhappy word or deed of mine, I pray Thee of Thy great mercy to heal and restore her, that she may serve Thee without hindrance.

I do not think you were ever maimed by any word or deed of mine. You lived too warm and full a life to have been maimed. But for the times that I hurt you, may I be forgiven. I cannot remember that we ever went to bed in anger, but if we did, may I be forgiven for that also.

34

May 25th, 1926. The anniversary of your husband's death. This day I may not see you or touch you or speak to you. I am sick at heart, and consumed with jealousy, of a man who is dead, and of the years of your life that are closed to me. I would understand now how such a thing could be, though I would not be that way myself. I look back with compassion upon you, and upon that young man who was myself, who after eight months of loving and being loved, must this day be cut off from you and from your life. He did not see the sense of it, he did not understand it at all. He goes to have his evening meal at the hostel, and they look at him with astonishment and speculation, because he has not eaten there for almost a year.

I did not mean to write this down. The book was finished and ready for the final typing. Then I thought to myself, *why leave it out? This is how it was, this is how you were, this is how I was.* So here it is written down.

35

We were married on July 2nd, 1928, in the Church of St John next to your home Morningview. I had bought my first tailor-made suits, one to be married in, and one to 'go away' in, according to the custom of those days. They each cost six pounds (twelve rands). After the wedding was over, we went to Morningview for the reception. There I drank alcohol for the second time in my life. The first time had been a year or so before. I was staying with Neville in Durban, and his mother being away, we decided to try the experience of getting drunk. For this purpose we bought a bottle of port, with no result whatsoever, except that we made ourselves shout at each other so that we would not feel that the experiment had totally failed.

It was a deliberate decision on my part to break with the teetotalism of my upbringing. It was also — may bishops forgive me — another step in the direction of Anglicanism. It was also a tribute to yourself, to the wholesomeness of your life, to a morality concerned with affirmations, not prohibitions.

36

It is over two weeks since I wrote anything. There is a reason for that. There is one more painful thing to be written, and I could not bring myself to write it, yet I knew that if it were not written, then I would not write anything more at all. And I wish above all else to write more. Therefore this one thing must be written.

We had decided – quite a decision in those days – to drive to Victoria Falls for our honeymoon. Our first night was to be spent at Howick.

I do not know when I first noticed that you still wore your first wedding ring, which you had moved to your other hand. When we went to our bedroom, I said to you, *are you still going to wear your first wedding ring?* To which you replied, *Yes.*

What did I do? And how did I feel? I cannot remember. I do not believe that anything I might write here would be the truth. So I must relate only those things that I know to be true. I must record here that whatever the pain, it was outweighed by the joy of being alone with you, of sleeping in the same bed with you, of fully loving you for the first time, of being in the same room with you, of knowing that you were now Mrs Alan Paton.

Of this pain I write now for the last time. I write about it because it is part of the story of our life. But it is only a hundredth part of it. I hope I shall never think about it again.

At the end of July 1928 we returned from our wonderful holiday, and after saying farewell to all our friends in Ixopo, we set up our new home in Pietermaritzburg, for I had been appointed, not only the form-master of IIIA, but also the first teacher of the new subject of Physics at Maritzburg College.

37

Anoxia of the brain. A lack of sufficient oxygen supply
to the brain. Your lungs struggle ceaselessly to supply
it, to oxygenate the blood, but in their present state
they cannot do it. Although you breathe in pure
oxygen twenty-four hours of the day, you cannot
breathe in enough of it to feed your brain. You wake
trembling and frightened, anxious over the new day
that has to be fought with and suffered and endured.
Most often you do not waken me; you lie with your
anxiety alone. But sometimes your hands' trembling is
uncontrollable and frightens you, and you ask me to
come to calm you. And my heart wishes to break, because it is not words you need, not love, but oxygen.
One morning I said to you, *I wish I could give you one
of my lungs.* But you did not even smile at me; your
fear was too great. You were like a woman on a
vanishing spit of island in a raging river, and I was like
a man on the bank, desperate but safe; I could not
touch you, and if I cried out to you, you could not hear.

Sometimes you were impatient with me. Once you
said to me, *I know I am a burden to you,* and when I
protested, you said, *I am a burden to you all.*

You wrote to Ruth on January 22nd, 1967:

I might say I'm such a hypocrite that when Dr
H. suggested a week in King George V I *meekly
and cheerfully agreed,* but as soon as he'd gone,
the storm of repression and depression broke loose
on poor Alan ... Really I deserve to be shot for

pre-judging so erroneously and grumpily, after all the blessings God has bestowed on me all my life.

Dr W. said to me, *You must expect such things to happen. Your wife cannot be blamed for it in any way. It is a condition she is powerless to prevent. She may even turn against you, and you must keep your patience.*

Once when Dennis and Devi were visiting us, the tape holding the catheter tube in place against your cheek became loose. I had fixed the tape many times, but this time you would not let me touch it. You said, *don't touch it, I want Dennis to fix it.*

If I did become cross or impatient, I was filled with remorse. I used to pray, with great earnestness, *Lord, make me the instrument of Thy love, and let me speak no angry or hurtful word.*

On March 17th, 1967, you wrote to Ruth:

I am trying hard to overcome my depression and regain my courage ... I know this will take time, but I am determined to make it work. I so long to be up and about again. Also when I do start getting up, I'm going to get dressed. Then I'll really feel on the road to recovery.

On April 2nd you wrote in your diary, 'Alan managed to come earlier. Feel so homesick when he goes.' On April 3rd you wrote, 'I am obviously lacking in determination and perseverance.'

You were not lacking in determination and perseverance, you were lacking only oxygen. You never lacked in determination and perseverance your whole life long. Everyone but yourself thought you one of the bravest of women.

38

Yesterday I found two books in my bookcase, *Gregg Shorthand* and *Gregg Shorthand Dictionary*. In the first is written 'D. Francis, May 1920', and in the other 'D. Francis', in the firm and beautiful handwriting of your youth. Although I did not know you then, the books brought back to me the halcyon days, the days that one has had and cannot have again.

Were you learning Nederlands too? At the back of the first book is a translation (in your own writing) of the limerick about Maud, the society fraud. It reads:

> Er was een jonge dame roep Maud
> Wie was een Societe skellum.
> In die bal-kamer hets verteld
> Zij was zeer, zeer, koud,
> Maar op die eerste landing, 'Allemachtig'.

The English version was something like this:

> There was a young lady called Maud
> Who was a society fraud.
> In the ballroom, it's told
> She was very very cold,
> But on the first landing, my Gawd!

You thought this was very funny. You liked a good story about sex, but you were chaste, as were all your sisters. You had no prurience in you. You were warm in love, but otherwise not demonstrative. I shall not easily forget the times when you showed your affection. They were mostly times when I had been away, perhaps for many months. I would leave the plane and walk across the tarmac looking for you. When we first saw each other your face would be alight with warmth and joy, and when I reached you you would embrace me with that fierce affection you kept for special occasions. When I remember them, I long for you bitterly.

39

December 7th, 1930. This day David was born. It was I who suggested that his second name should be Francis, your family name, and you were very pleased with this. The Buick was sent from Ixopo by your mother to fetch her grandson to Morningview; she would not hear of his making such a journey in a Chevrolet. It was my mother's first grandson, and my sisters' and brother's first nephew, and they were all very proud of him. So was your mother, especially when he began to give early intimations of his intelligence. So were you and I, but I was proud of another thing also, long since forgotten and only remembered since I began to write this book. One of your old family servants came to see you and your baby, and she said to you, *Miss Dorrie, you are looking so well.* And you replied, with that mischievous cocking of your head which you often used to accompany the saying of something serious, *it's because I have a good husband, that's why*.

There is an expression which I never use, *you slay me*. Well I shall use it now, and I shall say, you slew me then.

40

I have a secretary at last. I wanted to get one long ago, in the early days of the emphysema, but you would not let me. Then when you came back from all those months in hospital in June 1967, you started to type again, sitting there so thin and frail and brave. Sometimes you had to give up, because of the trembling of your hands.

My secretary has come to know you well, first through the letters that I write about you, mostly to people who have just heard, or who have written not knowing. Then I began to speak to her about you. Then came a letter from the editor of an American magazine saying that he was running a series called *Works in Progress*, and asking whether I was writing anything, and if so, would I send him excerpts?

I was moved by the impulse to ask my secretary for her judgment, and I asked her if she would like to read what I had so far written. She said she would and so I gave it to her. She reads very quickly, and when she had finished she said to me, *I never knew your wife, but she springs to life in these pages*. She said to me also, *you must certainly go on writing it.* One cannot say anything more pleasing to a writer than to say that the person he is writing about springs to life in his pages. I thought immediately of the picture of you playing reformatory bridge, and the picture of you telling me that you were determined to have a bath — *you must help me, Alan,* — and the picture of you angry with that anger of which one was never sure whether it was anger or not, and I am glad that I can make you live again.

I thought of sending four excerpts, the first one of the night and morning of your death, the second one which tells of our first meeting on the tennis-court, the one which tells of the reformatory bridge, and the one about the anoxia of the brain. My secretary says it is the saddest of them all, and it is. It is also the most terrible, because it brings home the truth that even the warmth of love depends on a material element called oxygen. This realization would have been unendurable for me had it not been for that same Francis of Assisi. He did not curse the cruelty of God for making leprosy, he came down from his horse and kissed the rotting flesh, *believing as he did so that he was mediating the love and pity of God.* He wrote in his will, 'the Lord himself led me amongst them, and I showed mercy to them, and when I left them, what had seemed bitter to me, was changed into sweetness of body and soul.'

This is almost beyond comprehension. It seems to suggest a God who has love and pity but no power, or it seems to suggest that that is the way the universe is, that God is both powerful and powerless, both Creator and Destroyer, that He can only atone for His cruelty by His love. It is altogether too difficult for me to comprehend. I can only endure the thought of it by holding the belief that the only way of atoning for the apparent cruelty of God towards men is by showing forth in one's life the love of God towards men. I suppose this may be blasphemy, but at least it is honest blasphemy. But perhaps it is not blasphemy at all, but an acknowledgment — first made centuries ago — of the incomprehensibility of God.

The thought also comes to me that not only the warmth of love depends on a material element called oxygen. The whole of life, the whole world of man and animal and tree, all activity, all the vast human accumulation of knowledge, all history, the whole terrestrial creation, all depend on it. The total lack of it brings all life to an end. The partial lack of it changes life drastically. But one seldom reflects on these things, until one sees them with one's own eyes. If it were a reflection occurring frequently, there might be no sudden realization of the truth that the warmth of love depends on a material element. And perhaps it is only when it happens to a person one loves, that this truth seems terrible.

Never during your long time of suffering did I turn against God. Among the times that I most gladly remember are the communions at your bedside, you most humble and devout in the worship of God, even though He did not abate your suffering. And I was humble too, knowing that however much I loved you, there were things you needed more than love, and they were beyond my power to give.

41

The joy of physical reunion. It was to me one of the greatest of all human joys. When I had been so long away from you in 1946–7, I wrote to you, *I want you to know that I have been faithful to you.* I landed in Cape Town after a thirty-day voyage from St John, New Brunswick, and was bitterly disappointed that you were not there. When I saw you on the platform at the Johannesburg station, your face was alight with joy. Lanky drove us to the house, and the moment that he left us, we were in each other's arms, loving and wordless. I think I whispered to you, *shall we have a bath?* and you nodded your head. And so we made love, after all those many months. I remember it now, not with sorrow, but with joy.

There was another such occasion, and I have been given permission to tell about it. When I returned from England in 1948, you and David (aged seventeen) and Jonathan (aged twelve) came to meet me in Durban. When we reached the hotel, I said, *I'm going to have a bath.* You said, *I'll come too.* Jonathan said, *I'm coming too.* David, who at that time ruled Jonathan with the elder brother's rod, said most emphatically, *You are not going too.*

I wish to write down here, that of all the beauties of creation, there is none more beautiful than the spirit and flesh of a chaste and loving woman.

42

On September 24th, 1946, I left Stockholm at 9.0 p.m.
by train for Norrland, and we turned west at Sundsvall
over the mountains that separate Sweden from Norway, through forest after forest of birch trees turning
yellow, and alongside of us a green foaming river like
no river that I had ever seen. Then down to Trondheim, where I arrived on September 25th, and the
girl at the desk of the Hotel Bristol could not understand what I wanted until Engineer Jensen came up
and translated for me. When that was done Engineer
Jensen said to me, *would you like to see the cathedral?*
and I said I'd be glad to.

It was four o'clock and growing dark and the cathedral, like all Norway, was very poor, so that the lights
had been turned off for the day. The engineer showed
me round the cathedral with a torch, and when that
was done, we sat for a long time in silence, looking up
at one of the most beautiful rose-windows in the world.
And I was homesick for you and my country.

We returned to the hotel at about six o'clock, and
the engineer said, *I'll call for you at seven, to take you
out to dinner*. And I sat there in my room, and out of
my homesickness I wrote those words, *there is a lovely
road that runs from Ixopo into the hills.*

When I landed in Cape Town in February 1947, I
brought back with me the manuscript of an unpubli-
shed book opening with those words, a book begun in
Trondheim, Norway, and finished in San Francisco,

California. I gave it to you to read, and when you had read it you said, *it is one of the most beautiful books I have ever read.* Its name was *Cry, the Beloved Country.*

So many things have been written about this book that I would not add to them if I did not believe that I know best what kind of book it is. It is a song of love for one's far distant country, it is informed with longing for that land where they shall not hurt or destroy in all that holy mountain, for that unattainable and ineffable land where there shall be no more death, neither sorrow, nor crying, for that land that cannot be again, of hills and grass and bracken, the land where you were born. It is a story of the beauty and terror of human life, and it cannot be written again because it cannot be felt again. Just how good it is, I do not know and do not care. All I know is that it changed our lives. It opened the doors of the world to us, and we went through.

You were proud of it but it hurt you too. You were hurt when insensitive people made a great deal of me and paid little attention to you. You were hurt when they remembered me but had forgotten you.

When you died, Susie wrote to me about the year 1946–7, when you worked together in Balgowrie House.

It was during that year when she worked for the Boys' Clubs and I for the Christian Education Movement that we cemented our friendship by lunching together daily. As we shared our hopes and fears, laughter and tears, the shy reserved person I had met revealed a sparkling wit and penetrating sense of humour, a clear and simple faith, and a loving heart. So I loved her dearly.

Susie then goes on to write about the way in which I led you into this strange new exciting world, but it would not be seemly to quote her here, except her last two words, *Laus Deo*. Which words I say after her.

I was in New York in 1949 when I heard that I was to share the London *Sunday Times* award with Spencer Chapman, who wrote *The Jungle is Neutral*. A special award was to be made to Mr Winston Churchill, for the first volume of his history of the war, *The Gathering Storm*. The *Sunday Times* wanted to know whether I would fly to London to receive the award, and I, feeling very rich after twenty-seven years on a public servant's salary, not only decided to do that, but cabled you to fly to London from South Africa, and then we would fly to New York for the play, and then we would fly to California to see the Burnses, and you were to buy all the clothes that you wanted.

Then I flew to London to meet you. For some reason I arrived late at the airport, and there you were sitting alone, waiting patiently for me, smart as smart could be. I was remorseful but you were radiant. We took a taxi back to my flat in St James's Street. And again, that wordlessness.

That was your first step into that new and exciting world. Though you took your first step into it bravely and apprehensively, in the end you conquered it, not by pomp or pretension, but by warmth and integrity.

Though you did not say such things often, you said to me more than once, *in my family I was the lucky one.* When you wrote in your diary of the many blessings you had received, you meant not only your house and garden, not only your sons and their wives and their children, not only those many journeys, not only the deep affection of so many people, but also that wretched person who wrote a book that so changed and enriched your world and his.

I can see you now, demurely sitting there alone, smart as smart could be, like a very small girl waiting to go to a very big party.

43

In 1934 I spent seventy-seven days in hospital with typhoid. In those days the treatment for typhoid was starvation, and I wasted away, losing fifty of my hundred and fifty pounds. Twice you came to take me home, because I was thought to have recovered, and each time they took my temperature, and sent me back to bed at once. The second time I broke down and wept; I thought I would never go home again. You hid your own disappointment, and tried to comfort me. Your preparations for my home-coming, in which kind of task you excelled, the special food, the books, the visits from family and friends, the hundred things you had arranged to give me pleasure, all came to nothing.

When at last I came out, I had great difficulty in walking. I sat in the garden in the autumn sun, and you waited on me, as they say, hand and foot. When I could walk, I went one day to town, and in Church

Street the father of one of the boys I taught at Maritz-burg College, stopped me and asked, *what are you going to do now?* I said, *I'm going back to school.* He said, *you won't stay there long; after an illness like that, you'll do something new.* And he was right. A few months after that I applied for the Principalship of one of the three reformatories, Tokai, Houtpoort, and Diepkloof.

In 1934 Parliament decided to transfer all reforma-tories from the Department of Prisons to the Union Department of Education, with the intention of re-placing a penal objective by a reformatory one. Our friend J. H. Hofmeyr was then Minister of Education, and applications for the three Principalships were called for in the Government Gazette. I wrote to Mr Hofmeyr telling him that I wanted to try my hand at reformatory education, and he advised me to apply for all three, Tokai for white and coloured boys in two separate institutions, Houtpoort for younger white boys, and Diepkloof for African boys of all ages from seven to twenty-one, seven being the earliest age at which a boy could commit a criminal offence. You agreed with great reluctance, hoping I would not get Diepkloof, especially as Mr Hofmeyr had written 'it is hard to know what can be done with it.' But that is what I got. I took the letter into the garden, and tried to summon up courage to tell you. When at last I told you, you were much distressed, and would not be com-forted. You said to me tearfully, *what do you know about reformatories? What do you know about African delinquents? Why do we have to leave Natal, where all our family and friends are? I don't want to go.*

That was one of the occasions when I could not go up to you and comfort you, because we were estranged by this event. It was only time in your life that you did not want to accompany me. You did not want to leave the security of Pietermaritzburg, and that countryside of mist and grass and bracken, you did not want to venture into the unknown world of the Transvaal and reformatories and delinquency and who knew what else. But I was excited about it. At the age of thirty-two I was being given the chance of turning a prison into a school, I was being given a school of my own. Up till my illness I had hoped one day to be made the headmaster of Maritzburg College, probably at the age of fifty. Instead I went off to Diepkloof at thirty-two, not soberly as I no doubt should have done, but a trifle light-heartedly. I am sure that none of this helped you to overcome your feeling of hurt, because I had, without visible signs of regret, overturned your world. It was more than a month before you followed me.

In later years you were to accompany me, bravely and loyally, on ventures far more dangerous than this.

44

July 1935. My first month at Diepkloof Reformatory, as foul a place as ever I saw. Four hundred boys were housed in wood-and-iron buildings set round a hollow square, one side of which was used for administration. Round the entire block, and about twenty feet from it, ran a thirteen-foot-high barbed-wire fence, inclining at an angle towards the building. In this block was a great gate, and opposite it was a corresponding gate in the high fence, and the two gates might not be open simultaneously, except when the whole reformatory marched out to work at 8.0 a.m. and 1.0 p.m. or when it marched back again at noon and 4.0 p.m. At the gates were men in uniform, and when I arrived they greeted me with quivering salutes, impassive faces, and a thundering of heavy boots on the concrete as they came to attention. The outside of the huge block was closed and blind, except for high windows heavily barred. Four hundred boys lived in the block in about twenty rooms, the doors of which opened on to the hollow square. Just after five o'clock in the afternoon, when they had had their supper, they assembled together for evening prayers, and sang as beautifully as any four hundred boys ever sang upon the earth. Then they paraded outside their rooms and were counted. Then they paraded inside their rooms and were counted again. Then they were locked in for fourteen hours, with one bucket full of water and another bucket for urination and defecation. The lights burned all night, and in each door was a spy hole through which acts of turpitude could be observed. The stench which poured out of the rooms when the doors were opened at 7.0 a.m. was unspeakable. The boys paraded outside their rooms, and were counted. After breakfast, which they ate sitting on the ground, they paraded, each in his appointed place. The group with which each boy paraded was called his *span*, which is the Afrikaans word for 'team' or 'gang'. Afrikaans was the language of the reformatory; most of the white personnel was Afrikaans-speaking, but above and beyond that, Afrikaans is, except in Southern Natal, the language of the African delinquent. It is a weird and wonderful Afrikaans, far from pure and certainly far from holy, but full of the vitality of the slums of the cities.

When all the boys had paraded with their spans, they were counted. If the count proved correct, the two gates were opened and the spans marched out to work on the reformatory farm, the numbers again being counted by the officer on duty at the gate. At noon they returned, and were counted in. After their midday meal they had half an hour of rest, and again, on the ringing of the bell, paraded with their spans and were counted, marched out with their spans and were counted, returned at 4.0 p.m. with their spans and were counted.

These countings, these locked doors, these double gates, and the high fence that ran round the whole block, had naturally one purpose and one only, and that was to prevent the inmates from running away. How was this one purpose to be reconciled with, or at least to operate alongside of, an educational and reformatory purpose? That was the problem that I had to solve somehow, for if I did not solve it, then I would have proved myself a fool for ever having undertaken to do so. And there was another problem, practical and urgent. What was I to do about those buckets in the rooms? It was unthinkable that I should allow such a thing to continue.

Meanwhile I was saluted and stamped at continuously. I was treated as though I were an emperor of some immense domain. Yet this was all a façade. Behind it sixty pairs of eyes were watching me, sixty men, some of them prison officers with many years of service, watching this young schoolmaster of thirty-two, who perhaps had never before seen a delinquent in his life, who could not have clapped a pair of handcuffs on anybody if he had tried, who had no doubt read many books in the silence of a sequestered study. How would he make of this grim foul padlocked encircled and potentially dangerous place, anything that might be called a school?

I now knew what Mr Hofmeyr meant when he had written 'it is hard to know what can be done with it.' I had only three cards of any value; one was an overwhelming determination to do something with it, the second was an aptitude for wrestling with problems, and the third was a physical energy that amazes me when I look back on it.

To this grim place, to the miserable small dark house allotted to the principal, to these at first sight intractable problems, you came some time in August 1935. You came because it was your duty, but you did not pretend to like it, this barred and alien and forbidding place.

45

I have just come back from Johannesburg, where I went to say goodbye to Bill and Margaret Hoffenberg, and to see our son David made a Master of Medicine in Diagnostic Radiology.

Bill was I think your second favourite, Peter your first. But you had so many I could not count them all. If there was anything that helped to restore your confidence in yourself, it was the Liberal Party and the friends we made in it. I think that without exception your friends were mine, though of course I did not look at the men in that gay mischievous way.

Bill looked as handsome as any prince, in a dark elegant suit. Margaret also looked smart, but one could see the strain in her face. Because Bill was banned, only one person could speak to him at a time; otherwise he would have been taking part in a 'gathering', and could have been arrested on the spot, and have spent his last South African days in prison. All the students lined up just outside the airport entrance, and Bill came alone across the road to them, and the student leaders went one by one to meet him, and each read to him a message from the student bodies. Bill accepted each of these messages in turn, shook hands with those who brought them, one by one, not all together, and then walked slowly down the line, all of us clapping, and Bill smiling slightly, raising his hand repeatedly, all this without self-consciousness, but with extraordinary dignity and grace.

When we were all back in the airport building, I went to say a brief goodbye to them both, brief because I had seen a great deal of them that day and the evening before. Although nothing was said, we were all three thinking of you. I said to the *Sunday Times, I hope to live to see the day when they return to us,* but it was a wish rather than an expectation. Weep for yourself, South Africa, that you can do such things to your sons.

The next day was more cheerful. To celebrate David's degree we all gathered at the Salonika for dinner, a real Paton dinner, though I notice that Jonathan's boyhood appetite is beginning to decline. Do you remember that when he was a boy he would try everything on the menu, and when he flagged, David would say, *come on, bring out the forces?*

We made one mistake however. On Saturday nights at the Salonika the minimum charge, exclusive of wine, is four rand per person, and this we failed to reach. Why, we could all have had caviar or smoked salmon! When we discovered our mistake, no one had any forces to bring out.

This was the second Paton dinner we have had since you left us. Something has gone, but something also remains.

46

What was I to do about this unspeakable stench that poured out of every dormitory when the doors were opened at 7.0 a.m.? Could I continue to be the principal of such a 'school' as that?

So, watched by those sixty pairs of eyes, I decided not to lock the dormitories at night, so that boys could visit the lavatories when the need arose. I also decided that all the dormitories would not be opened at once, but that they would be opened at the rate of one each week.

The first three weeks were not anxious ones. Out of four hundred boys, at least sixty were mere children, of ages ranging from nine to fourteen years of age, the great majority having committed simple and not very serious theft. They were almost without exception docile and obedient, and eager to please the emperor of their domain. They occupied three of the dormitories, and these were opened on the second, third and fourth Mondays respectively of my principalship. When all the other dormitories were locked at 7.0 p.m. these small boys would rush round and round the interior space which was called the Yard, whistling and yelling and skylarking, delirious with their freedom, until the first and second silence bells rang at 9.0 p.m. and 9.05 p.m. It was my intuition — perhaps not very well founded — that three hundred and forty other boys, listening to this tumult, were looking to the day when they too would be free, but I knew that some of my sixty men looked with fear to it, when this same freedom would be given to boys who had robbed with violence, and had grievously assaulted, and had raped and murdered, many of them not boys at all, but young men, made hard and tough by the life and ways of Kliptown and Pimville and Orlando and Sophiatown, young men who could bludgeon watchmen and scale walls and kill those who stood in their way. And if a dozen of them ganged up together, and murdered the officers on night duty and took their keys and went out into the dark countryside to rob and kill, well the possibility was terrible to contemplate, but it had to be contemplated. There was only one way in which to guard against such a possibility, and that was to create a strong arm of law and order inside the reformatory itself.

To do this I enlisted the help of my staff. I asked them to select from their spans boys with gifts of leadership and personality, one or two for each of these twenty dormitories, these same boys to be the officers' seconds-in-command in the spans, and to enjoy a measure of freedom not given as yet to others. Those boys who were chosen for promotion were called head-boys, and were given a bright red pocket on their shirts. Promotions were made at the daily evensong, and the boy being promoted came out and faced the entire congregation, promising in a clear voice not to leave the farm without permission, not to touch any property not his own, and to carry out quietly and willingly any duties allotted to him. Later — I cannot remember when — the whole reformatory would clap in congratulation.

Another thing had already happened that lightened the heavy and sullen atmosphere of Diepkloof. On the first Thursday of my principalship I came back to my office after lunch to find half of the reformatory lined up outside my office, and I said to Captain Stewart-Dunkley, formerly of Poona, and now Chief Warder of Diepkloof, *what's all this about?* He replied in his impassive military manner, *Thursday afternoon, sir, is Offences Day*. I said in astonishment, *but what have they all been up to?* He replied, *most of them, sir, have been smoking*.

The Secretary for Education at that time was Professor M. C. Botha, the son of poor parents, yet destined to become one of the most distinguished of South Africa's public servants. He was my boss, and no man ever had a better. He had told me that he was there to help me in what would be no easy task. I went into my office, and telephoned him. I told him that half the reformatory was lined up outside my office, and this was apparently a weekly affair, and that most of them had been caught smoking. Professor Botha said to me, *you can issue tobacco tomorrow*. I went out to my Chief Warder and said, *tobacco will be issued tomorrow*, to which he replied in his impassive manner, *very good, sir*, and marched off all the smokers, leaving me with a handful of boys charged with more serious matters, such as smoking the weed called *dagga* or *insangu* (called in America marijuana), committing some homosexual offence, assault and so forth.

The announcement at evensong that tobacco would be issued to all boys of sixteen and over, and a ration of sweets to all boys under sixteen, was greeted with something very like cheering, only muted, because such a demonstration was unprecedented. The atmosphere of this grim fortress was changing, and some of the sixty approved, and some did not. Each Monday another dormitory was opened. On the ninth Monday of my principalship eight dormitories were open.

47

Now at night one hundred and sixty boys were free till 9.0 p.m., to run about the Yard shouting and singing, to form their choirs and bands, and to paint pictures on the whitewashed walls of their open dormitories, pictures such as I have never seen before. There were pictures of boys with stolen handbags fleeing from the cops, of planes and cars and trains, of the streets of Johannesburg both rich and poor, of courts of justice with august magistrates on the bench and naughty boys in the dock. Some boy from Durban would paint a nostalgic picture of the ocean, and a boy homesick for the country would paint an idyllic picture of cows and horses and birds, in a meadow under a willow, weeping into some river of home.

Some of the staff disapproved of this freedom and this activity. Some were honestly afraid of it. If things went wrong, think how badly they could go wrong, with one hundred and sixty boys enjoying the freedom of the Yard, and three unarmed men on night duty, carrying, not weapons of defence, but the keys of the main gates and the doors of twelve yet unopened rooms, containing two hundred and forty boys who were in general tougher and more mature than those already freed. To these doubters on the staff, this freedom and these choirs and this liberty to paint pictures on the walls were bribes and sops, and their acceptance depended upon the whims of boys who had already shown themselves to be wayward and inconstant. But to me these new things were the signs of the beginning of a new order, where life would not be kept under lock and key but liberated under discipline, under the discipline not only of the laws, but of the new selves that would burgeon when they were made free to paint and sing and shout, and to decide whether or not they would begin to live in obedience to the laws.

I was fortunate that at least half of my staff saw these new freedoms, not as bribes, but as the beginning of a new order, dangerous to bring about, but, if it could be brought about, constructive and healing.

Yet I, guardian of the wayward and inconstant, was at that time wayward and inconstant too.

48

In the week following that ninth Monday of my principalship, you suddenly said to me, *Are you in love with Joan?* And I said, *yes.* You said, *what are you going to do about it?* and I said, *stop it.* You said, *Surely she must be consulted about it,* and I said, *we have already spoken about it.* Then I said to you, *I ask only one thing, and that is to go down to Natal and say goodbye to her,* to which you replied, *I am willing that you should.* Later that day, or that night, you said to me, *what did I do wrong?* But I cannot remember what I answered, or if I answered at all.

I do not find this easy to write about, but it must be written, because this book is about you, and what I am about to write tells something very important about you.

Joan was a university student whose mother had also come from Ixopo, and she was often in our home in Pietermaritzburg. She and I got on well, both of us being devoted to English literature. Our friendship grew stronger and deeper, but it was only I who knew consciously what was happening to it. And I could have stopped it, but I did not.

Did I fall in love with her because she was young and beautiful? Was I taking some revenge, or giving myself some reparation? Whatever I had done, I had no wish to lie or temporize when you asked me your question. I was not ashamed of loving her, though I knew it was wrong of me. When I answered your question, was I just being honest, or did I wish to hurt you?

When I left Pietermaritzburg to go to Diepkloof Reformatory, I was in love with Joan, though no one knew it but I. But soon after you arrived at Diepkloof, she came to Johannesburg to play hockey, and she came to stay with us. I would take her into Johannesburg in the mornings, and go to fetch her in the afternoons or evenings. It was on one of these return journeys that we admitted our love for each other. When she returned to Pietermaritzburg we wrote daily, and I found a reason to go down to Natal for a long week-end. It was not long after that you asked me your question. You had not found any letter or handkerchief or memento, you knew by intuition.

The next day after you spoke to me, or perhaps the day after, I drove down alone to Natal to say goodbye to Joan. Both she and I knew that what we were doing was wrong, and it troubled us; therefore it was a relief and a pain to say goodbye to each other. I watched her for the last time open the gate of the house where she stayed, and walk up the path, and let herself in at the door. She turned and gave, hardly a wave, but something more like a sad salute. So it came to an end. It was a brief encounter, but I dreamed about her two or three times a year till the year that she died.

The next day I drove back to Diepkloof, subdued and quiet. You met me at the door of the house, and you took me into your arms in that fierce way of yours, and you held back your head so that I could see the earnestness in your face, and you said to me, *I am going to make it all up to you.*

I do not know when I noticed that you were no longer wearing your first wedding ring, but that night when we went to bed it had gone from your finger. All I know is that when you died I searched the house for it. Strange, is it not, that if I had found it I would have treasured it? It is a strange story altogether, isn't it? But it is a true story of life, and if I lived it again I'd like to live it the same way, only better.

That was the beginning of our Diepkloof life, thirteen years of disappointment and achievement, of failure and success, of happiness and fulfilment, and of labours prodigious and now almost unbelievable, and an ever-deepening love of an institution and its four hundred wayward boys. It later grew to five hundred, six hundred, seven hundred, and some people said in all seriousness that the Education Department's policies were making reformatories more attractive, and that boys were committing crimes in order to get into them.

We were to spend at Diepkloof thirteen of the happiest years of our life. I am reminded today of what Francis of Assisi wrote in his will:

> The Lord himself led me amongst them, and I showed mercy to them, and when I left them, what had seemed bitter to me was changed into sweetness of body and soul.

In a humbler way it was true also of us.

You said to me, *I am going to make it all up to you.* There could not have been many women like yourself.

49

When I went to the reformatory block the next morning, my vice-principal met me with a solemn face, and told me that he had closed all the open dormitories while I was away. He said that he had not felt able to bear the responsibility of having one hundred and sixty boys free in the Yard.

Was he giving me notice that he could not support my policies? Or was he, after half a lifetime spent in the Prison Service, with its discipline and its rigidity, unable to adapt himself to this programme of change and experimentation? Or was he just plain afraid? I think the last was true, so I did not reproach him. Instead I took a step which in retrospect seems to me to have been extraordinary. I gave orders that every dormitory should be opened that night.

I spent the first part of that evening in the Yard, amidst a noise indescribable, of laughter, shouting, home-made music, singing. Several times I made a round of the Yard, being greeted with the Afrikaans *goeie naand, meneer*. At nine o'clock the first silence bell was rung, and four hundred boys went to their rooms. At five minutes past nine the second bell was rung, and the silence was absolute. I went home and you looked at me with anxious inquiry. I said to you, *it's going to be all right*. And you said to me, *I think so too*.

There were other things that gradually won your heart. Although the reformatory block was one of the ugliest places in the world, the reformatory farm was one of the most beautiful. There were many plantations of eucalyptus and two of pines, these last containing venerable trees, under which was a thick carpet of needles, golden and fragrant. The orchard, mainly of peach trees, yielded an abundance of fruit as choice as any in South Africa. Beneath the picturesque stone kopjies of Comptonville lay the terraced vegetable gardens, acre upon acre of tomatoes, cabbages, beans, peas, pumpkins, marrows, carrots, lettuce, potatoes, all of which the staff could buy for a halfpenny a pound.

There was another thing also. David, now five, took to the reformatory as a duck to water. It was his day-time home. After a while he was made an honorary staff-member, and in the afternoon would march out his own span of twenty small boys, who all called him Da-véed. This not only helped to make you feel that Diepkloof was your home; it did something else too. It helped to persuade four hundred boys that something new was abroad. Gradually the appellation *die tronk* (the jail) fell into disuse and was replaced by *die skool* (the school). The Department itself took similar action, and the warders now became supervisors, while the inmates became pupils. I, who had come as Warden, now became the Principal.

One of the results of the opening of the dormitories and the removal of the buckets was that the reformatory latrines could not cope with the new demands, and I urgently petitioned the Department to build eight new ones. Within a few days — thanks to my boss — a contractor arrived and built them. He was barely gone before another contractor arrived to build eight more. Someone in the Department had slipped up, but I said nothing. I was later reproved, but meanwhile we had acquired a brand new double set of latrines which were kept spotless. This had one important consequence. Typhoid fever, which had been the scourge of the reformatory and the cause of many deaths, almost completely disappeared.

50

Yesterday, Good Friday, Margaret and I went to the three-hours' service. It was taken by Lloyd Wellington, the Dean of Pietermaritzburg, in a new and striking way, for it was a narrative, related in the first person by Longinius who was the centurion who carried out the Crucifixion. Thus the seven words from the Cross are more than words, they are events in the life of a hardened soldier who comes to realize that he is in the presence of no ordinary man. I have never found it so easy to listen to the seven meditations. Alas I wept more than once, partly because of the majesty of the story, and partly because you were not there. Good Friday, though a solemn day, was always the most peaceful day of our year. A quiet morning, the three-hours' service, then lunch and a walk round the garden, and music in the evening. May you, whatever your place or condition, be at peace also.

51

It was not only the typhoid that disappeared. Gone were the shouting, the anger, the rebuking, that had been the outward signs of the hidden conflict between age and youth, between officer and boy, which is the mark of every bad school, penal or otherwise. The new recruits to my staff came from the Special Service Battalion, and it was a proud thing, and it remained a proud thing for thirteen years, to see one of these young men move to the bell, and to hear the whole yard, which had been full of cries and laughter, fall absolutely silent, each boy moving to his place. It was not only the sudden transition from pandemonium to silence which was a proud thing to hear, but just as proud was the equally electrifying transition from silence to pandemonium, when the parade or ceremony was over.

I suppose that these young men had had these gifts

of personality before they went to the Battalion, but the Battalion undoubtedly perfected them. One does not like to single one out, but there was a *primus inter pares*. This was I.Z., a young man of six foot four, with gifts of personality out of the ordinary. I took him away from routine work, and told him that I wanted to give to every boy who had completed nine months a measure of physical freedom, and this was to increase step by step until the boy was physically totally free, and could abscond whenever he felt like it. For I clung to the belief — which was at that time founded on faith — that you could not cultivate a sense of purpose and responsibility unless it were accompanied by physical freedom, and that the granting of physical freedom would prove far less dangerous than one feared.

These young men had no tradition of prison service. They knew that they were participating in an exciting experiment, which might succeed or fail. What a waste it would have been of their lives and talents if they had had to devote themselves to the drudgery of ensuring that no one ran away!

Our house became their home. You could not speak Afrikaans, so that they spoke to you in English. You treated them as you treated most younger men, in that gay and mischievous way of yours. We played Monopoly and bridge, and it was then that we developed the game of 'reformatory bridge', which you thought I played so meanly. All your fears disappeared, and Diepkloof, that alien and forbidding place, became our home and the home of our sons for thirteen happy and purposeful years.

·–[103]–·

52

Elizabeth came to see Jonathan and Margaret on Easter Day. We asked her to stay to tea, and she hummed and ha-ed, and said the taxi was waiting for her. When we insisted, she said she would have it in the kitchen, and when we objected, she consented to have it with us, and did so with as much constraint as you could put on a five-cent piece.

She was as racy as ever, and laughed when I reminded her of the days when she was with us. I asked her if I could tell the story of them, and she said, *I don't mind, God knows it all.*

When you came back from hospital in June 1967, Dr C. said you must have attention day and night. For the night we engaged Queenie Ngubane, and I made inquiries about someone for the day. That is how Elizabeth came to see me, a big strong coloured woman who called me *master*, but quite clearly had a mind and personality of her own. She said, *there's one thing you must know, master, I'm not one for beating about the bush, I've got three children and I'm not married, but perhaps I'll have to get married because there's no coloured school for my children, you see, master, if I get married then my children will be Indian children, and they can go to school in Wyebank.*

So Elizabeth came, Roman Catholic by religion, with an earthy wit, and kind and strong and patient. Soon after she started work, Murray came to give us communion, and when I knelt at your bedside, I was astonished to see Elizabeth kneel there too, and communicate also. When Murray was leaving, I said to him, *do you know that you have given communion this morning to a Roman Catholic living in sin?* Murray said to me, *if she wants it and she needs it, she can come.* I said to Elizabeth teasingly, *how can a Roman Catholic join in an Anglican Communion?* Elizabeth said, *Ag, there's only one God, isn't there?*

One day she asked you for the day off, because she wanted to get married and become Mrs Pillay, so that her coloured children could become Indian children, and go to school in Wyebank. A few days after she brought us the wedding photograph. I said to her, *why do you look so glum when your husband is all smiling?* Elizabeth said, *Ag, what's there to smile about?* And I remember another time when I had been dressing in our room, I came out to find Elizabeth standing waiting until I had finished. I said to her, *Elizabeth why don't you sit down? What are you standing up for? To be good?* And she replied, *Master, it's too late for that.* And I remember of course the last time of all, on the morning that you died, how when I told her she ran through the house to your bedroom, as though she might catch a glimpse of you before you left us finally.

Our thanks to you, Elizabeth.

53

I could not foresee in 1935 that the consequence of increasing the amount of physical freedom would be to reduce absconding drastically, to change the atmosphere of the reformatory from one of grimness to one of industrious gaiety, and almost to eliminate the feelings of anxiety and tension. I was too deeply committed to see that the setbacks were only falterings in a ceaseless moving forward. I passed through periods of despair, and said (rather than prayed) to God, *don't You want this to happen? Because if You don't want it to happen, I'm going back to a safer job.*

But apparently He did want it to happen. I remember the first time boys were signed out of the Main Gate, and I remember it well because you came yourself too, to wish me luck. Of every hundred of these boys, one absconded on the first occasion, one within the next four weeks, one before the time for his release. Ninety-seven did not abscond at all.

On New Year's Day, 1936, we took away the front portion of the high barbed wire fence and the second great gate that was in it. At first it was like being naked. I became known, in a limited way, as 'the man who pulled up the barbed wire and planted geraniums'. Why geraniums I cannot remember, because I do not like them much. If I planted them, it must have been because there was nothing else.

54

Sue spent the morning here and read this book, and after that we talked about you for a long time. In four days it will be six months since you died; grief is gone, yet I think about you many times a day. This very day I had a letter from someone who had just heard of your death, and another yesterday.

Sue told me how cross you had been with her during last year's preparation for my birthday party, because she told you that you were not to worry about anything. How you resisted letting anything go! I suppose you were holding on to life. How reluctantly you gave up the croquet! And the walking. And then, with sad and silent acceptance, the bath. And then the typing. But one day you were going to take them all up again, when you were better, and had been weaned from the oxygen, and had reached the end of this long convalescence that was eating up so much of your life. Even when the cancer struck at you, you regarded it as an unfortunate setback that would make this long convalescence even longer. Then began the heavy injections, so that your doubts and longings were stilled. Sometimes you would start whispering, and I would get out of my bed and come to listen to you, hoping that it was some last message, of love maybe, but I could never make out what you were saying. I told Dr C. that I longed to know what you were saying, and he replied, to comfort me perhaps, that you were saying nothing. What were you saying, my love? What thoughts were passing in your mind, now closed to us?

On your last Tuesday night an astonishing thing happened. David and Jonathan and I had gathered as usual in your room for our evening drinks. Then on that night you suddenly came to, put on your glasses, and picked up the newspaper. I wrote out the word puzzle for you, and you took it, but you could not make a word, and if you could, and you wrote it down, no one could read what it was.

I thought that was the last time you had been aware of us, but Jonathan reminded me that I was wrong. On your last Saturday, less than forty-eight hours before you died, Archbishop Paget came to see you, and you said to me very sharply, *Alan, don't keep the Archbishop standing, get him a chair.*

It is strange that a person at times so diffident could be at others so sharp and confident that she would be obeyed. You said to David and Jonathan in the sternest and most emphatic way, *if your father wants to get married the day after I die, neither of you is to say a word.* Even though you were living with three persons whose characters were as strong as your own, you would brook no encroachment on what you considered to be your territory. If you became angry, it was no use trying to appease you. You would throw up your arm to keep us, as it were, at arm's length, saying, *don't come near me, I'm angry and I'll stay angry if you do things like that.* And if one of us said, *I shan't do it again,* you would relent, with something that was between a smile and a pout.

As with your anger at reformatory bridge, we would not have had you otherwise.

55

July 6th, 1936. On this day Jonathan was born. I could not go to see you both, because on that day I contracted German measles, the only childhood disease I have ever had. The matron had a ladder put up against your window, and I climbed it every day to see you and your son. David and Jonathan – a risk to take – but it turned out all right. The arrival of Jonathan was the beginning of what one might call our family life. I could not wish it had been happier.

56

On September 11th, 1967, you wrote in your diary,

A. told me he must get away for some nights from our bedroom, as I'm getting him down. This has been the unkindest cut of all, whether or not I deserved it. My only peace is oblivion.

And under it I wrote,

A sad passage, but Dr C. advised me to do so. Do not think I told D. that she was getting me down.

On September 12th, you wrote,

Made up A.'s bed in spare room and he accordingly moved out. Hope he'll now have more peaceful nights. Feeling desolate but am trying to be realistic and fighting against it. Faith is so weak. If only I could rest in God.

On September 28th, in St Augustine's Hospital, having developed cancer, but not knowing it, you wrote,

A. phoned several times re homecoming arrangements. Both of us edgy. Why?

Later on the same page you wrote,

A. and I still edgy with each other. Depressing.

Under this I wrote,

A sad passage, but I was not aware of edginess. Dorrie complained bitterly about the hospital. This may have made me edgy. Dr H. told me anoxic patients do not know what effect their actions have on others.

On September 29th, back at home, you wrote,

Glad to be out of hospital, but I have still not learnt to accept. In fact I am becoming less and less long-suffering. Utterly ashamed.

and later on the same page,

Queenie turned up with incipient cold . . . Q.'s cold was last straw to my endurance. I infuriated A. and drove him out. However peace was eventually restored.

That night I returned to sleep in our room but you did not note that in your diary. However there was a consolation. Three evenings later I had to go into

Durban to speak at the Gandhi birthday commemoration and did not expect to be back till 11 o'clock. But when I had finished speaking, I felt it was urgent to go back home. I arrived at about 10 o'clock, and when I walked into the room, your face lit up with pleasure and you said *what a pleasant surprise!* That was at a time when you almost never smiled.

For the edginess, the desolation, the impatience, for all the things that could have been done better, for all the things that should not have been done at all, I do not ask forgiveness, because I know they have already been forgiven.

57

April 23rd, 1968.

Six months today since you left. I was supposed to wake at a quarter past five, and leave the house at a quarter past six for the airport to fly to Johannesburg to speak at a meeting to protest against the Bill, which, when it becomes law, will make the Liberal Party an illegal organization because it opens its membership to people of all races.

I woke at half past two, and went to sleep again, after reminding myself that I had to wake at a quarter past five. But I didn't. When I woke it was almost seven, and I knew I would have to take another flight. And then I remembered. In memory I could hear Queenie saying to me, *father, she's gone.*

I cannot remember when I last overslept. Was I wanted in the house on this morning, or was it I that wanted it? Was I wanted in the house at the half-anniversary of that day when your body was taken away, never to come back again, never to be seen again, never to be loved again? Or was I wanted to be here, so that instead of spending the morning talking politics in Johannesburg I could write this message for you?

Tell her, O gracious Lord, if it may be, how much I love her and miss her, and long to see her again; and if there be ways in which she may come, vouchsafe her to me as a guide and guard, and grant me a sense of her nearness in such degree as Thy laws permit.

Yes, I love you and miss you this day. My grief that I wrote was gone is renewed for a while. I remind Theresa and Anna that it is six months since you went. I ring your sister Beryl and remind her too, and she weeps and says *Oh Alan it's a long time.* Yes, it is a long time. I think of you today almost continually, of the halcyon days, and the countryside of hills and grass and bracken, and the titihoya crying. And the journeys and the jokes and the teasings, and the word-less reunions, and the pride in your sons. And I weep too, for myself, for the days that will not come again, and for this sudden return of pain. Are you guarding me today? Then guard me well.

I shall have to leave for the airport soon. The last time I was there, to meet David and Jonathan, a woman and three children were there to meet the plane. And a man came through the gate, and picked up the three children one after the other, and hugged and kissed them. When he had put the last one down, he went to the woman and put his arms round her and kissed her. And when he had kissed her, they stood cheek to cheek in each other's embrace, so that I could see her face. And it was alight with love and joy. And I said to them in my heart, *Yes, I know.*

I must leave for the airport now, but I don't want to go. I want to spend the day in this house, which somehow does not seem empty now. I want to write for you, but instead I have to go to Johannesburg and write a speech.

58

Why is it that grief should suddenly return after exactly six months? Why does one remember more intensely at anniversaries? Before the calendar was invented, did men and women remember more intensely on any particular day? What happens if one's wife dies on February 29th? Will grief return to me on October 23rd, 1968?

These are idle speculations, and not very profitable. What I am really thinking about is the astonishing fact that I went on sleeping for one and a quarter hours after I should have got up, and that after booking for another flight and after telephoning Jonathan that I would arrive later, I thought of you continuously, and wrote for you a piece that makes me weep when I read it. Have you read it too? Then you cannot doubt that you were loved. Sometimes on earth you did. Once when you were in such a mood, David said to you, with a sharpness worthy of yourself, *what are you moaning about, with your beautiful house and your beautiful garden, and a husband who loves you?*

Well, I went to Johannesburg, and at a packed meeting in the Darragh Hall I made what many people said was the best speech of my life. And yet in a way I wasn't there. I have come to the conclusion that one makes one's best speeches when one isn't there. But I was sufficiently there to say to Ernie Wentzel, who said I had made the best speech of his life too, *why, haven't you heard me speak before?*

We had another Paton dinner on Wednesday night. Jonathan brought out the forces and ended up with *crêpes suzette*. And on Thursday I flew back, and went round the garden to see how much things had grown in forty-eight hours. It is going to be beautiful in two months' time. The verge is planted with dwarf candytuft, eight hundred of them! The Wise bed is planted with self-coloured pansies, six hundred of them. The one croquet-lawn bed is planted with dwarf dianthus, and behind them your flowers, the St Joseph lilies. The other three beds are planted with calendulas, stocks and dwarf phlox. The Hemphill bed is planted with dwarf phlox also. And on the front porch are little pots, with alternating red and blue achimenes. Sue congratulated me on the garden, and I told her of the day I came home and found it strewn with papers. It had obviously been done deliberately, and I couldn't understand it. But I did understand it when I saw you watching me from the front door, with that strange mixed look of defiance and mischief on your face. *Did you do it?* I called.

And you replied, *I did.* I said, *what on earth for?* And
you said, *to teach you a lesson. When you stop leaving
books and papers all over the house, I'll stop putting
papers in the garden.*

Really, for a woman in her sixties!

59

On New Year's Day, 1937, I removed the remaining
three sides of the barbed-wire fence surrounding the
reformatory, and again for a few days had that feeling
of nakedness.

Then the Department built four free hostels, and
later four more, each looked after by an African teacher
and his wife, and each housing twenty-five boys. These
were boys who had used their freedom well, and they
were now allowed home leave once a month. Of every
hundred who were allowed this leave, one would not
return, one would return late, one would return under
the influence of liquor. Ninety-seven returned, prompt
and sober. The absconding rate, which had been eleven
per month, dropped steadily year by year, and when
we left in 1948, it stood at three per month.

The Department permitted a drastic reform in my
first year. Up till then every boy when he left was
apprenticed to a white farmer for the unexpired portion of his retention period. This practice was now
abolished, and one of the results of this was the intro-
duction of workshop training for all those occupations
open to African boys. Most of these shops we built

ourselves at first, out of wattle and daub, with thatch for the roof. We made our own shoes, tailored our own clothes, did our own tin-smithing. Other boys were trained in building and laundry work. About one hundred boys still worked on the farm, mostly those from rural and agricultural areas, and another hundred were trained in nursery work and horticulture. The gardens of Diepkloof became known for their beauty.

All four of us, you, myself, David and Jonathan, were lovers of Diepkloof. The young men, both white and African, came to identify themselves with the new methods completely, as did many of the older ones. It was almost impossible to believe that Diepkloof had once been so harsh and forbidding.

Not all were impressed by this change. One of our critics was Dr Hendrik Verwoerd, then editor of *Die Transvaler*, who described Diepkloof as the place where one said *please and thank you to the black misters*, and dismissed the educational programme, the system of increasing responsibility and freedom as *vertroeteling* (pampering). When he became Minister of Native Affairs, he had the responsibility for African boys transferred to himself, and closed down Diepkloof altogether, and transferred its boys to different parts of South Africa, according to their ethnic grouping, where the practice of working for white farmers was re-introduced. *

Many people asked me if this did not break my heart.

---

* One of these ethnic units was established at Thabanchu, and in 1968 its headmaster told a friend of mine that there was talk of introducing trade training, but 'these things take a long time'. Thus after thirty-three years, *vertroeteling* is coming back.

No it did not. What would have broken my heart would have been to have had to stay there, under a Minister with whom I had almost nothing in common. He would have discharged me or removed me, and perhaps have embittered my life. For this I have to thank that strange event, the writing of a book which captured the hearts of so many of the people of the world.

So we left Diepkloof, you weeping, and I, shut up in my office sobbing for the first time since my childhood days. So ended those thirteen years.

60

When I left Diepkloof I cherished several illusions. One was that I was going to become a writer, one of that lucky breed who lived in California or Maine or Cornwall, and had no responsibility to the world beyond writing about it. Another strange illusion was that I would never wear a formal suit again. So we went to live first at Anerley, then at Southport,* and stayed there for five years.

At seven in the morning we would go to the beach. What you said was true, that it meant something special to you to feel the touch of water on your body. In the water you were more like a child than a woman, and swam about with a look of bliss. Then you would lie on your back and throw water over yourself. After the swim you performed your drying ritual, and when

* Seaside resorts seven miles north of Port Shepstone, Natal.

that was done, you must have said, five hundred times at least, *that was beautiful.*

It is a good thing to go home after a morning bathe to breakfast and the newspaper, and then to walk through a meadow of flowers to the post office for one's letters. In September *Cry, the Beloved Country* was published in England, and the volume of correspondence doubled. We would spend the morning at this, and in the afternoon, after a siesta and tea, we would walk for an hour inland, or to the sea, and sit for many minutes watching the green swells running to the land, then lifting themselves into great walls, which reared themselves higher and higher until they crashed down with a sound of thunder, their white manes streaming away in the wind. We would spend the evenings reading and you would do a great deal of knitting. There were no signs then of the dread emphysema.

During these years of idyllic life, I left you several times to go to London and New York, and would return to see your excited face at the airport. But it was not a writer's life. In fact I lacked what may be the supreme gift of a writer, and that was not to feel obliged to do anything but write, and to want to do nothing else but write. I wrote *Too Late the Phalarope* in Cornwall and *Meditation for a Young Boy Confirmed* in a cabin in a redwood forest in California. *To a Young Boy who died at Diepkloof Reformatory* I wrote at Anerley. Yet all the time I was being drawn back into that world of action I had tried to leave.

It was at Diepkloof that we began to feel that the colour-bar that ruled South African life was unendurable. So far as we were able we threw it out of our own lives. Into our circle of friendship were drawn more and more people of other races and colours. Yet meanwhile the Government more and more set its face against inter-racial relationships, clubs and associations. In Cape Town, Durban, Pietermaritzburg and Johannesburg, there were people who felt it was time to establish a Liberal Party which would espouse openly the inter-racial and non-racial ideals, and would do so in the political field.

We began to feel more and more that we could not go on living the idyllic life. Yet when we left we did not go directly into politics. We went to work for a year at the TB Settlement run by Toc H at Botha's Hill, under the inimitable Don McKenzie, who, as the Warden of an institution for the sick and the crippled, had no peer.

It was during this year that the Liberal Party was established, and when I left the Settlement it was to become the National Chairman of the Party. None of us could foresee that the establishment of such a party was gradually to attract to itself the hatred of much of white South Africa, and to become the cause (with other organizations) of the passing of more and more restrictive legislation, the imprisonment without trial during the emergency of 1960 of many of its leaders, the banning and restriction of their movements, the prohibition of their participation in any social gathering (even a dinner party), and finally their exclusion from this or that occupation, which forced many of them to take exit permits to leave the country, never to return.

What does one do when one finds oneself up against the might and power of the State? No one knows how awesome this is until it happens. Then one must decide either to pull out or to go on. Though you at times were apprehensive you had no doubt that we ought to go on.

So we went on.

61

Yesterday we held the last meeting of the Liberal Party at Hambrook in Northern Natal. On Tuesday we shall hold the last meeting in Durban. On Wednesday we shall hold the last meeting in Pietermaritzburg, which will also be the last meeting to be held in South Africa. All this because the Government will shortly make it illegal for a white person and a black person to belong to the same political party. We could have re-formed of course, into a white Liberal Party, and a Black one, and a Coloured one, and an Indian one, and that would have been to adopt the very policy of racial separation that we came into being to oppose. These last meetings were resolute, but inevitably sad, and they are made more sad for me because for fifteen years the Liberal Party was the greater part of our life. Why you, from your country home, and I, from the quiet streets of Pietermaritzburg, each with a typical white South African upbringing, should decide to challenge the conventions of our white society, is a mystery and a miracle. Is it not strange that you and

I, all our lives till then blameless before the law, should find ourselves followed by security police, and have our telephone tapped and our letters read and have our house searched, and receive threats of death, and anonymous letters that were almost without exception obscene, and have a security policeman sitting in hotel dining-rooms, watching us eat as though there was a danger that when we swallowed we might swallow the Army and the Air Force and the Government and all?

To you, wherever you are and in whatever condition, I send thanks for all your faith and courage, for all your help and encouragement, for all that strength of character that conquered your fears and that clearness of mind that could tell a cruel deed in spite of all its wrappings of noble words. How you would have ridiculed the hypocrisy of our white indignation because these naughty Olympic nations won't let our white boys and black boys run together in Mexico, when we ourselves won't let them run together in Johannesburg. On all sides one hears that we have been 'shabbily' treated.

I remember when the security police came to search our house on March 19th, 1966, you were in bed and not well. They were quite courteous until I left your writing-room and went into the bedroom to tell you they were there. Then one saw the other face. One of them was after me in a flash, and said to me peremptorily, *you will return at once, and you will not move again unless you are given permission.* I said to him with extreme coldness, *this is my wife's house, and I am telling her who you are, and what you are doing*

·–[121]–·

here. I returned to the writing-room and sat on the big chest, not angry, but in that extreme coldness. I know nothing more distasteful than to watch a stranger going through one's papers, and reading letters that one thought private to oneself, and behaving as though it was he who owned the house.

You could have stayed out of it all but you did not. When you came, dressed, out of the bedroom, you looked exhausted and ill, but people were searching your house, and reading your husband's papers, and you wished to be there. It was time for tea, and you asked the police if they would like some. You and I sat in one corner of the lounge, and directed them to the tray. When they had poured their tea they brought it over and sat with us, and we made conversation about dogs and the weather and the asthma of the wife of Captain X, who thought you had asthma too. After tea they asked to be taken to my study, so I took them there and said to them, *Gentlemen, you may believe me or not believe me just as you wish, but this is where I write when I get a chance to write, and there are no political papers here*. So they didn't search the study.

Was I not lucky to have had such a person to accompany me, sometimes with fears but always with courage, along the dangerous road that one walks when one challenges the customs and conventions of a colour-bar society? I remember the words written to me by one in prison, 'she went your road — not an easy one — with willingness, courage, and it seems to me, ungrudging love.'

There is something else that I remember. Late one night in April 1960, during the emergency which was declared after Sharpeville, the telephone rang, but when I picked it up, no one said a word. An hour later there was a knock on the bedroom window, and I said *who's there?*, and a woman's voice answered, *it's me, Nancy*. What was our daughter-in-law doing there at that time of night? You were filled with alarm, and I was apprehensive. I let Nancy in, and took her in to see you. You said, *Nancy, what's wrong?* Then Nancy told us that she had been sent urgently by the Party in Johannesburg to tell me that the Party had been told by a 'reliable source' that I would be arrested that day. Ambrose Reeves, Bishop of Johannesburg, had also been told that he would be arrested, and, advised by some of his friends, had gone to Swaziland. Now the Party members in Johannesburg wanted me to be warned, but they did not advise me to stay or to go. They were very wise, because I had already decided not to go. I knew that in no circumstances could I go. And when I told you I could not go, I could see that you knew also that I could not go. Where did your courage come from? It was your religion of course, that strange Christianity of yours that took seriously the story of the Cross, that understood with perfect clarity that one might have to suffer for doing what one thought was right, that rejected absolutely that kind of Cross-less geniality that calls itself Christianity.

In those days no passport was required for Swaziland, so I decided to fly there by private plane to see the Bishop. Before I left I wrote out a statement for the Press in case I should be arrested before I could reach the airstrip. It was one of the best things I ever wrote, because I always write better under the influence of emotion. I don't know where it is now, but if I find it, it will go into this book. No one came that day to arrest me, and when I left at dusk I gave the document into your safe-keeping. You hid it on top of one of the cupboards in the guest bathroom, but as you lay in bed it became oppressively clear to you that when the security police came, they would go straight to the top of the cupboards in the guest bathroom. So you took it down from there and put it into your rolled-up red-and-white umbrella hanging up in your dressing-room. Then back in bed it became equally clear to you that when the police came, they would go straight to your red-and-white umbrella hanging up in the dressing-room. Then you had an inspiration of genius (which admittedly was based on the assumption that the security police were all gentlemen), and you took the document and taped it to your stomach, and then got back into bed.

When I returned, you told me this with gaiety and pride, as though you were hopefully inviting me to admire you, which I did, though in retrospect I see that I could have done it better. In retrospect I see that I could have done many things better.

62

It was clear when I arrived in Swaziland that the Bishop wanted me to tell him that he had done the right thing. Therefore I told him that he had done the right thing, for the reason that during the state of emergency he would be more useful outside the country than in, whereas I would be more useful in than out. I regret that I did so. I regret that I did not urge him to return to Johannesburg, that I did not tell him that there are crises in our lives where the criterion of usefulness is not the most important. Yet in a way I could not, because it had become almost impossible for him to return. The Church might have forgiven him, but the world would have not. To this very day it troubles me to think of him, which I do with much affection. To me he had a deep understanding of the gospel teaching. This led him to challenge the assumptions of a colour-bar society and to expose its cruelties. This caused him to be hated more than it caused me, because while, in the estimation of some, I was a born idiot, he was a foreign one.

63

On December 3rd, 1948, our friend J. H. Hofmeyr, Deputy Prime Minister of the Union of South Africa, the man who had sent me to Diepkloof Reformatory, died at the age of fifty-four. I decided to write his life, and you and I started on our travels (interspersed with travels abroad), to Cape Town, the city of his birth and his parliamentary activity, Johannesburg, where he had been appointed Principal of the University at the age of twenty-four, and to Pretoria, where he had lived as Minister of State for fifteen years. And of course, to a dozen other places.

You were my amanuensis, and took shorthand notes of all the interviews with people who had known Hofmeyr in many different capacities. Then the work was brought to an abrupt end when his mother, then eighty-seven, who had already complained that the work was taking too long, objected to my going to Scotland to see three retired professors of the University of the Witwatersrand, on the grounds that she had told me all the facts already. I said to her, *Mrs Hofmeyr, a biographer must go to see many people, so that he can hear all sides of a story*. She did not answer, but she knew that the argument was unanswerable, but she said to you, *M-my son f-finished the biography of Onze Jan in t-twelve months, when he was only eighteen*. You replied, *Mrs Hofmeyr, this will not be that kind of book*, a reply which she clearly did not like. When we left, she said to me, *I don't think we'll meet again*, and she was right because we did not. She lived for ten more years, and it was only after her death that we thought we would be able to resume the task, but one political crisis after another, including the National Emergency of 1960, made this impossible. At last the leaders of the Liberal Party more or less ordered me to give up active work, and complete the book. This took another two years, and much of this time we spent at Halley Stott's beautiful cottage at Ramsgate, Natal, where we bathed in the sea pool every morning at seven, worked till lunch time, slept and walked in the afternoon, and did jigsaw puzzles in the evening.

In 1963 we travelled to and from Cape Town several times, to have the book edited by Leo Marquard. The single journey was eleven hundred miles, and each time we tried a different route. It is hard to believe that you could do and enjoy all these things in 1963.

So at last the stupendous task was finished. *Hofmeyr* was a book quite different from *Cry, the Beloved Country*, but in other respects I rank them as equal. When the book arrived at last, I inscribed a copy for you,

To Dorrie,
from Alan, author, husband, and boss.

You were not the only one who concealed deep feelings in light words.

64

Our last Liberal Party meeting in Durban's Caxton Hall was packed out, largely because of the large number of students. Dots, Pondi and Florence were there, and all three of them said you were there too. I told the meeting that the fifteen years of the life of the Liberal Party had enriched your life and mine beyond computation, that once this had happened to one, one couldn't go back again. With what fear, what excitement, what rationalizations, what reservations, one approaches the forbidden door, and touches it, and opens it a little, and shuts it again, and then finally opens it and goes through and shuts it against oneself, and enters into a new country whose very dangers and anxieties and adversities become resplendent in this new and shining and exciting light. One's self has been remade, and one can no longer return to the self that one was before. Nor does one wish to do so, except in times of extreme depression. One knows one cannot, because one could not live with such a self any more. I have known people who have returned, and they live always on guard, just as Peter was on guard in the palace yard lest yet another person might come and say to him, while the mob was spitting in the face of Christ, *why, weren't you one of them too?*

I remember once that you wept a little for the self that you had left behind. I had just been visited by a senior security policeman — it was in 1961 I think — who wished to know whether I always worked at home, whether I needed to visit libraries, whether I went to church and at what time I went, whether I needed to travel inside South Africa for my work, and similar questions. They were ominous, and pointed to some kind of house-arrest. When the policeman had gone, you came to me full of apprehension, and when I had told you what it was all about, you wept against me (which you did not often do) and said, *what shall I do if they take you away?* And I said, *they won't take me away, on the contrary, can't you see they're trying to keep me here?* My answer comforted you, and your question pleased me too, because you did not tell me often enough (for my liking that is) that my being there was something of great importance to you.

65

I remember too the time, when in a fit of unadmirable frustration I said to you in a manner also quite unadmirable, *do you know what I'm going to do? I'm going to join a brotherhood so that I can get out of this miserable world.* You began to weep, and said to me piteously, *Alan, but that would be the end of our married life.* And I was so ashamed to have made you weep, that I took you into my arms and said, *Sorry, dear, for talking so foolishly.*

But I was secretly proud to have seen you weeping. What children we are, always wanting to be loved, always wanting to be told that we are loved! Yet to love and to be loved make up for it all, for the pain and the frustration and the suffering and even the watching of suffering. That was the lesson that life taught to me. That was the lesson that life taught to Smuts also, for when his friends the Gilletts seemed to him excessively perturbed over the problems of the world (as he himself had so often been) he wrote to them, 'The children in the sandpit are the real thing.' *
Is to say such a thing merely a sign of age? Is it a proof that one has opted out? I don't think so. Young people, immersed in the activities of life, have told me the same thing.

To love and to be loved, they make up for it all.

* *Smuts: The Fields of Force*, by W. K. Hancock (Cambridge University Press, 1968).

There are some who would call this a dualistic view, and they would say that I should write, 'they are it all'. Well, I shall not. They are the wages that were paid to me for having had to live, and except on rare occasions, I never wanted higher. Sometimes I wish — especially when I am listening to erudite persons — that I could have had erudition also, but I know I can't have it now. It is the goal above all goals that one must start working for when one is young. How could I have done that in the halcyon days, with you loving me and hurting me, with that unspeakable joy of living with young and eager minds? And waiting for me, Diepkloof and that resplendent land beyond the forbidden door? One cannot have both erudition and the world. You always thought me erudite, but I was not. I had only a lively jackdaw mind, with traces of eagle and owl.

66

On July 4th, 1964, the security police conducted country-wide raids, covering a wider field than ever before. This time they raided members of the Black Sash, an organization of brave and public-spirited women, whom no one except the most fanatical could have believed to be carrying on any subversive activity. There can be no doubt that in part at least, the raids were intimidatory, and were intended to give notice that not even respectable women with eminent husbands could with impunity defy the State Almighty.

A number of members of the Liberal Party were searched and questioned, but one, whom I shall call Lester, was detained.

Lester's detention was the beginning of a series of dramatic events. Victor disappeared from Cape Town and was next heard of in England. Then Lydia of the same city was detained, and Dick was taken away from the conference of the National Union of Students in Pietermaritzburg, and also detained. Harold was detained in Johannesburg, and later Philip. Rita escaped to Swaziland, but there she was kidnapped by persons unknown and brought to Johannesburg, where the security police arrested and detained her. During the month one member after another was detained, in Cape Town, Durban, Port Elizabeth, Grahamstown, Johannesburg and Pretoria. It soon became known that Lester had broken down under questioning, and had informed on his associates in an organization called the A.R.M., the African Resistance Movement. Its members were all young people, some members of the Liberal Party, some ex-members, and some members of other organizations or of no organization. Its aim was to bring about a change in the government of South Africa by the use of violence and sabotage. Its members no longer believed in the use of non-violent weapons such as political parties, public meetings, house meetings, committee work, statements, demonstrations, protests, letters.

Lester's breakdown under questioning was not the sole source of the information gathered by the security police. He had actually kept a list of members of the A.R.M. in his room, and when he discovered that the police knew the names of all his associates, his resistance collapsed.

We had grown so accustomed to the harassment of the police that at first we did not believe that the raids were anything more than intimidatory. When we realized that an underground movement had been uncovered, and that it involved some of our own members, we were profoundly shocked. Up till that time the word 'sabotage' had been a word like any other. Now it acquired a grim meaning, for some of our own friends were going to be charged with it, and the punishment could be death.

At no time had I any evidence that Lester was planning sabotage. All that I had was the evidence of my own intuitions. One Sunday morning in 1963, when in Cape Town for a Liberal Party Conference, I had gone to Camps Bay for a picnic, and Lester was there, with Eldred, and one other young man not known to me. They all wore dark glasses and sun-bathed together in a place apart. They talked a great deal together, and went into the sea together, and came out of it together and went back to their sunny place together. Though there were many other groups on the beach, all the others seemed part of the crowd; only this one seemed separated. I, knowing nothing, thought to myself that they might as well have put up two poles and stretched a canvas across them with the red word, CONSPIRATORS. This intuition was made stronger when later at the conference Lester made an impassioned and deeply emotional speech, not advocating directly the use of violence, but pouring contempt and anger on our naive belief that we could achieve anything by non-violent means. A disturbing speech, not only because the man who made it was disturbed, but because the rest of us were disturbed also, both by the ugly realism of it, and by the realization that such an issue could drive a wedge between the younger and the older members of the party. For when you are embattled, driven back into the fortress, what is more to be feared than division within?

I spoke to Lester the following day. *Lester, I want to say two things to you which you may not like, but it is my duty to say them. The first is that if you are contemplating violence, you must not stay in the Party. The second is that if you are contemplating violence, you are making a great mistake, because you are not temperamentally suited for it and it can bring you only to disaster.*

What Lester replied, I cannot now remember. What could he say to me? He was too honest to say to me *I am not plotting*, and he dare not say, *I am plotting*. He was under oath to his organization to reveal nothing under any circumstances, even in face of death. But in his wounded pride he would have liked to say to me, *How do you know what I can do and cannot do? Wait and see.* I remember now the tortured and defiant face, of a man being driven inexorably by a force beyond his control, into a future full of fear rather than promise.

In spite of all these events the atmosphere within the Party was not one of recrimination. Though these young men had done such damage to us, and had done it under the cloak of our membership, our members hastened to the aid and comfort of their wives and children. Not one was excluded. On the contrary they were drawn more closely into the bravest fellowship that I ever encountered on this earth. And the young men, though they were in prison, were drawn in too. No one did more to draw them in than you. You understood with perfect clarity that though these young men, while still members of the Liberal Party, had embarked upon a foredoomed campaign of sabotage, their motive (or should I not rather say, one of their motives?) was a deep concern for the emancipation of all South Africans from the bonds of poverty and unjust laws.

I can see you now with them, in the days when you were well, with your head back and that mischief in your eyes. Thirty years ago I would have been jealous, but I had learned to harbour no jealousy at all, and indeed to write the words, *sex no doubt, but wonderful.*

It was in that company, not only of those young men but of all the others too, that you attained your fullest flowering. You were so fully accepted, and in time so deeply loved, that the hurt of having a famous husband was in great measure assuaged. You would still say to me at times, *you can't bluff me, they come to see you, not me.* I suppose this was true of most of those who came from other countries, but it became less and less true of our own circle. And their affection grew into respect when they saw the courage with which, in the days of your affliction, you presided over your house.

' ... blend of loved elder sister and mother ...'
' ... she was able to be gay because she knew, without vanity, that she was staunch and fine in the important things ...' ' ... Her strength came, not from denying the bad, but from affirming the good, which is why

young people (who feel their flawed character keenly, whatever they might pretend) loved and honoured her, and liked to be near her.'

I shall not easily forget these words, nor shall I ever forget our fifteen years' membership of the Liberal Party of South Africa, which though said by many to be unrealistic, naive, quixotic, impractical, sentimental, subversive, Communist-dominated, anti-Afrikaner, and many other things, enriched and deepened our lives to a degree incomputable.

This is a story that has two endings, one sad and redemptive, the other sad and terrible. For Lester, after less than forty-eight hours in the hands of the Security Police, not only uncovered the activities of A.R.M. but agreed to give evidence against his associates, many of whom he had himself recruited. He was taken round from court to court, and from city to city, to testify against his friends, so that they could be sentenced to three years, five years, ten years, fifteen years. He was taunted by counsels for the defence for his perfidy. In one court he broke down, and lifting up his arms to ward off the remorseless questioning, he cried out, sobbing, *My God, Apartheid is so terrible, I did it only because Apartheid is so terrible.*

When his job was done, he was given an exit permit, a document which allows one to leave but never to return. They promised him freedom if he would betray his friends. Did he not know that there can never be freedom for one who betrays his friends? Or does it happen perhaps that in solitary confinement and under those blinding lamps and under those hard unwinking unpitying eyes, one thinks that only to be free of them would be freedom enough? Does it happen that under the barrage of those ceaseless, ceaseless, ceaseless questions, one thinks that if only they would cease, then all questions would cease?

My friends, having judged Lester once, do not wish to judge him again. Many of us wonder how we ourselves would have stood up to that confinement, those lights, those eyes, those questions. Many of us would wish that even if Eldred, James, and Howard and Desmond cannot yet be freed. Lester could now be freed from the unforgiving past.

After Lester left South Africa he wrote to me:

Nothing I can say or do, now or in the future, can *ever* reduce the immorality of my decision — in spite of whatever reasons I had, which I have to live with and come to terms with ... I judge myself — and judge harshly.

I did not reply to this letter, not knowing where to reply to. But some years after, I heard he was in England, and having found his address I wrote to him. He has no religion, but I could not write to him in other than religious terms, because what I had to write to him about was nothing less than the forgiveness of sins. How can one write about that except in those terms? Who forgives sins except God and the person I sin against? There is only one other person who can forgive me, and that is I myself. But to forgive myself when I know no God, and when I am separated from those I sinned against by prison walls and thousands of miles of ocean, is surely impossible. Therefore I took it upon myself to say that those whom Lester had sinned against had now forgiven him, and that I did not know of any one of us who had not forgiven him. Therefore he must forgive himself.

The important thing to learn about sin is not that nothing can reduce the sinfulness of past sins. What is important is that they can be forgiven, and that once they are forgiven, one must at all costs forgive oneself.

67

July 4th, 1964. A dark and stormy night, and a clap of thunder that knocked me down in front of my own house door, so that I thought I would never have strength or courage to get to my feet again. That was the night that Jack came down from Johannesburg to tell us that John Harris, who had been taken in for ninety days by the Security Police in what we thought was only a further step in the whole process of intimidation, was almost certainly the man who had placed the bomb in the Johannesburg Railway Station, which so seriously injured an elderly woman that she later died, and which severely mutilated a young girl.

As it happened, John Harris was not then a member of the Liberal Party. His freedom of movement, speech, communication and employment had been drastically restricted, largely because of his work to ensure that South Africa should not be allowed to compete in the Olympics until she dropped the colour-bar in her own internal sport. There is no doubt in my mind that it was because of this restriction that John

Harris turned to violence as the only solution left, the only way in which to cause the Government to revise its unyielding doctrines of Apartheid and Racial Separation. Furthermore, because of his restriction he could no longer belong to any political party, and therefore strictly speaking it was not a member of the Liberal Party who had placed a bomb in a public and much-frequented place.

There was not however much consolation in that. What would the newspapers say? They would say 'Mr John Harris of Johannesburg was today arrested and charged with placing a bomb in the concourse of the Johannesburg Railway Station. Mr Harris had been a member of the Liberal Party.' Some paper might say, 'Mr John Harris had been a member of the Liberal Party up until the time of his banning.' And what help would that be?

I went heavily into the house, where you were waiting, wondering, worrying. And I went to you and said, *Jack has come to tell me that he is almost certain that it is John Harris who put the bomb in Johannesburg Station.* And you clung to me, full of fear and distress. And I clung to you, for I was afraid also.

And what or whom did we think of next? It was Ann Harris and her infant son. But they were already taken care of. The Hains in Pretoria had already sent for them in Johannesburg on the receipt of the news that John Harris had been arrested, and there they were to stay for the rest of their South African life, Ann Harris outwardly serene and tranquil, and her son kicking and innocent.

I wrote in *Contact*:

Nor will one easily forget the courage and generosity of the Hain family. They made a home for Ann Harris and her infant son the moment the arrest became known, and were her comfort and support throughout those terrible months. One need not say what construction cruel people put upon this act. The Hains disregarded such malice; they saw a job to be done, they thought it right to do it, and they did it well. These words apply equally well to Ruth Hayman, who applied herself to her tasks with characteristic unselfishness and zeal.

In this crisis, and in the other crises of 1964, the Liberal Party behaved itself in a way that it can be proud of. It condemned the deeds and it forgave the doers. One cannot do better than that.

68

It was not long after I went to Diepkloof, when after being a Warden I became a Principal, that my salary shot up from six hundred pounds to nine hundred pounds. Such an increase was fabulous to us. I think I raised your monthly allowance from two pounds ten shillings to five pounds! And we bought new furniture.

However, the greatest thing that happened to us was that we began to travel, first in our own country, and then further afield to Southern Rhodesia (now Rhodesia), Northern Rhodesia (now Zambia), Mozam-

bique, Nyasaland (now Malawi), Kenya, Uganda, and
to crown all, a trip with sons and daughters-in-law
from Durban to the northern boundary of the Ituri
Forest, a trip which included Elizabethville, Albertville
and Lake Tanganyika, Bukavu and Lake Kivu, the
volcanoes and Ruindi National Park, the equatorial
highlands and Butembo, and then to the foot of
Ruwenzori which came out of the clouds and showed
itself to us for ten exciting minutes, then to the caves
of Mount Hoyo and the pigmies, and the Ituri Forest.
Then we turned tail and made for Durban as fast as
we could, back to duties and appointments. Seven
thousand miles in a month, and never to be forgotten.

Your routine on these journeys never varied. You
got up before any of us and prepared for the road.
When we started off, you would settle down to doze.
Then you would hand us each something to eat from
your basket, which contained biscuits, sweets, apples,
a knife, knitting, and the road map. After we had
eaten you would turn to your knitting. When you had
had enough of it you would read the newspaper, with
an unconscionable amount of tearing, rustling, patting,
and the paper coming to pieces and being put together
again, as often as not cutting off the view of the driver.
Then it would be time for apples, which you would
peel for us. In between these various occupations, you
would be asked for information from the road map,
which sometimes you condescended to give with a
good, sometimes with a bad, grace. You would assume
an air of offendedness if you thought you were being
asked for information too frequently. On one occasion
you made the remark which became famous and which

was repeated to almost everybody. You were busy peeling apples, and I asked you how many miles to So-and-so, whereupon you said with asperity, *I've only two pairs of hands, haven't I?*

Of such small things was happiness made.

In later years these holidays became too arduous for you, and later still, if you went out in the car, the oxygen had to come too. You said to me, *You don't understand, you just cannot understand, how much I long to be able to go out without the oxygen.* Yes, I understood, only too well. You longed to go to Salvador's too, but you couldn't. One day I lunched at Salvador's with Bill Toomey, and on the way I called in at King George V to see you, and you wrote in your diary, *I nearly gave way to self-pity. I really must learn to accept.*

Then suddenly your old self would return. I was wheeling you round the garden in your chair, and I said to you, *I'm going to plant stocks there, and calendulas there, and take out all the balsams — we have enough anyway.* And you said to me, *Yes, you told me all that yesterday.*

69

Once before I wrote that my grief was done, and then it suddenly returned, on April 23rd, 1968. But now it will not return again. Something within me is waking from long sleep, and I want to live and move again.

Some zest is returning to me, some immense gratefulness for those who love me, some strong wish to love them also. I am full of thanks for life. I have not told myself to be thankful, I just am so.

And the book is done too, this Kontakion for you departed. I am glad it came to be written. It has in some strange way refined some dross out of me. It has taught me — though this was not my first lesson — to accept the joys and vicissitudes of life, and to fall in love again with its strangeness and beauty and terror. I have set down here my green and foolish hurts in those days when you loved and tormented me, and I shall never shrink from them again. As I wrote earlier, it is a strange story, and now it is done.

I have made my song, alleluya. And may you rest where sorrow and pain are no more, neither sighing, but life everlasting.